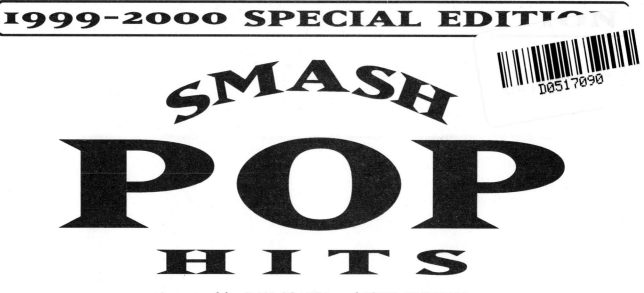

1999-2000 SPECIAL EDITION

SMASH POP HITS

Arranged by DAN COATES and JOHN BRIMHALL

Arranged by Bill Galliford:

ALL STAR

ANYWHERE BUT HERE

I'LL STILL LOVE YOU MORE

LOST IN YOU

NO SCRUBS

SMOOTH

SPECIAL

STRONG ENOUGH

THANK U

Project Manager: Carol Cuellar
Cover Design: Martha L. Ramirez

CONTENTS

AMAZED

Words and Music by
MARV GREEN, AIMEE MAYO
and CHRIS LINDSEY
Arranged by DAN COATES

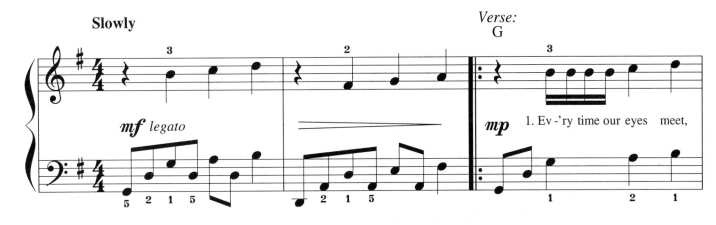

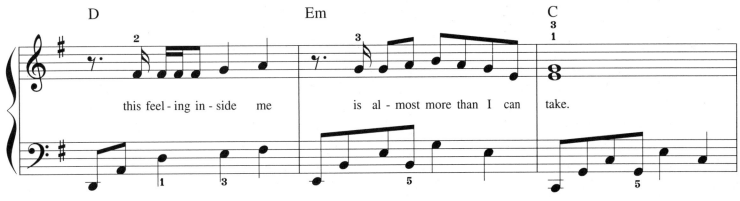

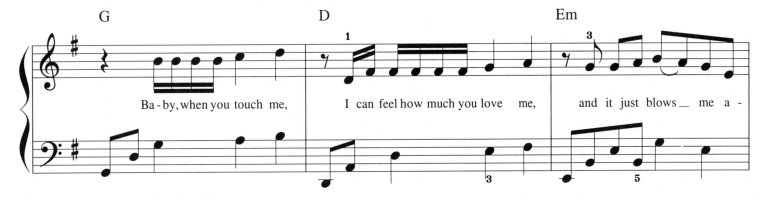

Amazed - 5 - 1

Chorus:

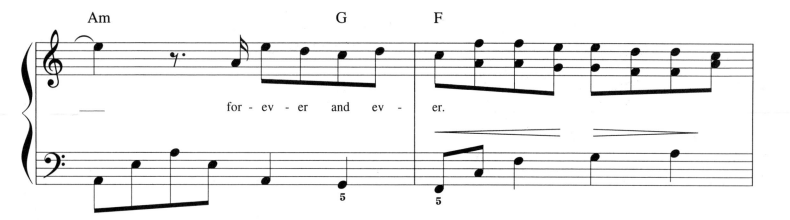

for - ev - er and ev - er.

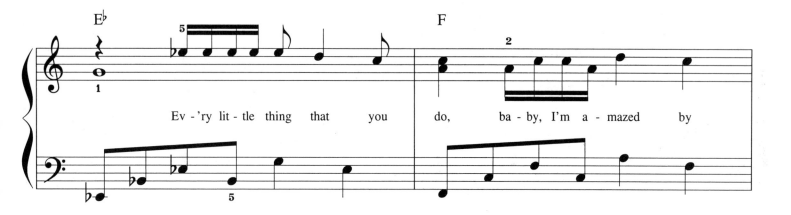

Ev -'ry lit - tle thing that you do, ba - by, I'm a - mazed by

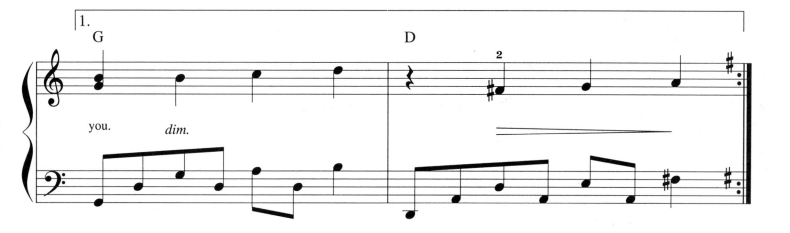

you. *dim.*

you.

mf

Amazed - 5 - 3

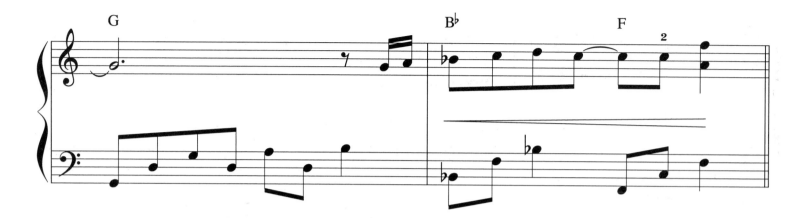

Ev -'ry lit - tle thing that you do, _____ I'm so in love with

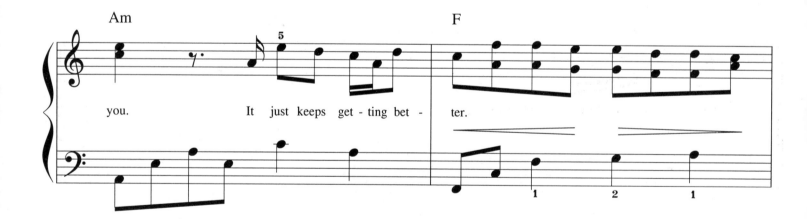

you. It just keeps get - ting bet - ter.

I wan - na spend the rest of my life _____ with you by my side _____

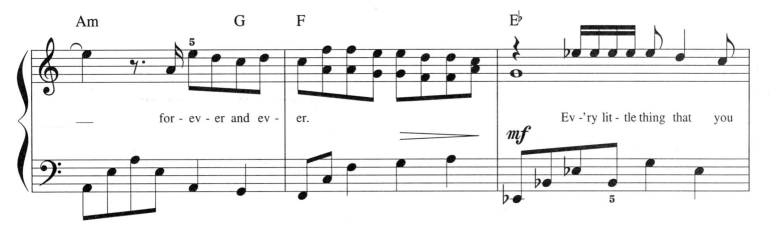

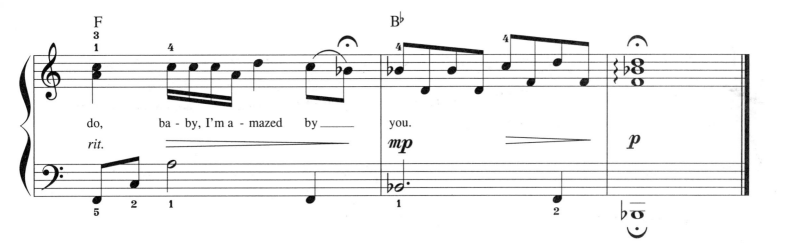

Verse 2:
The smell of your skin,
The taste of your kiss,
The way you whisper in the dark.
Your hair all around me,
Baby, you surround me.
You touch every place in my heart.
Oh, it feels like the first time every time.
I wanna spend the whole night in your eyes.
(To Chorus:)

ALL STAR

Words and Music by
GREG CAMP

Moderately (♩ = 100)

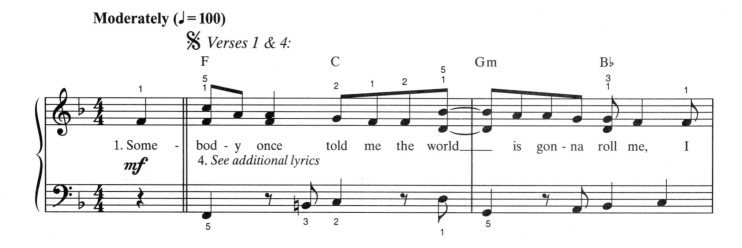

1. Some - bod - y once told me the world is gon - na roll me, I
4. *See additional lyrics*

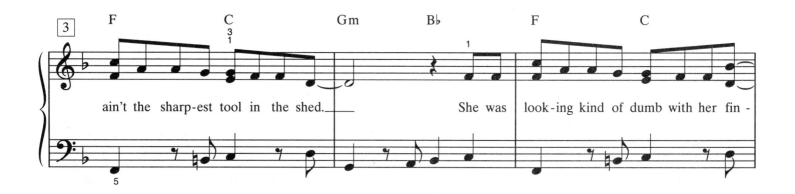

ain't the sharp-est tool in the shed. She was look-ing kind of dumb with her fin -

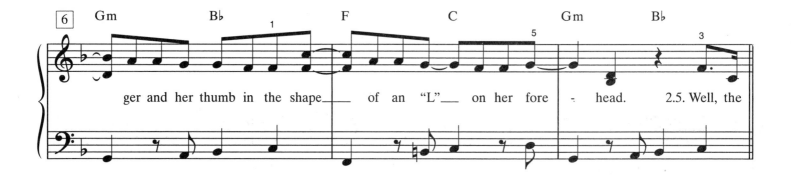

ger and her thumb in the shape of an "L" on her fore - head. 2.5. Well, the

All Star - 4 - 1

Verses 2, 3, & 5:

years start com-ing and they don't stop com-ing,   fed to the rules and I hit the ground run-ning.
3. *See additional lyrics*

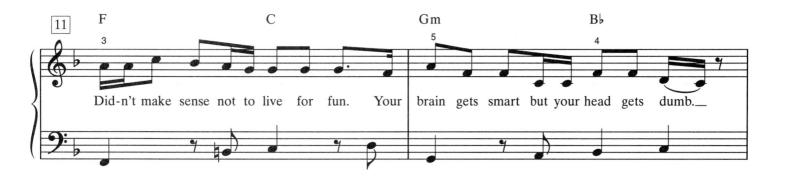

Did-n't make sense not to live for fun.   Your brain gets smart but your head gets dumb.__

So much to do, so much__ to see, so what's   wrong with tak - ing the back streets.   You'll

nev - er know if you don't go.   You'll   nev - er shine if you don't glow.

Chorus:

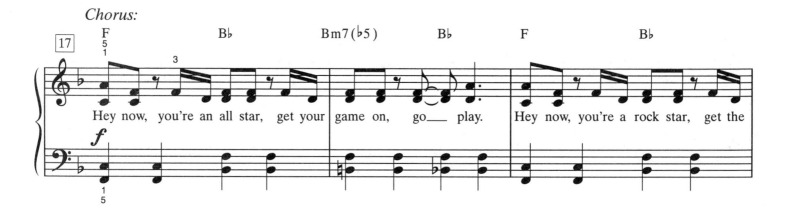

Hey now, you're an all star, get your game on, go___ play. Hey now, you're a rock star, get the

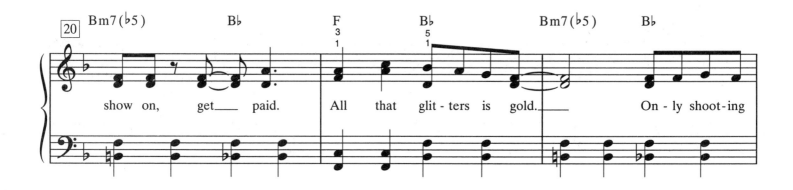

show on, get___ paid. All that glit-ters is gold.___ On-ly shoot-ing

To Coda ⊕ | 1. | 2.

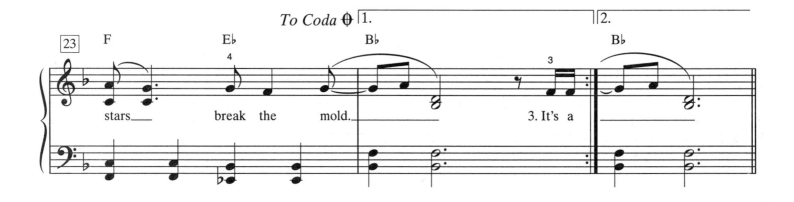

stars___ break the mold.___ 3. It's a

And all that glit - ters is gold.

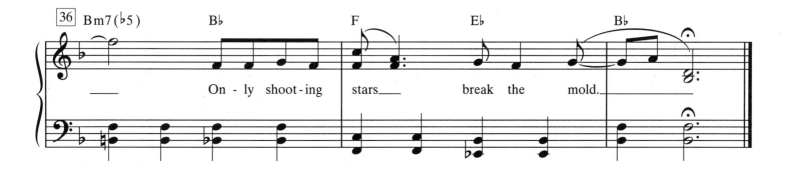

On - ly shoot - ing stars___ break the mold.___

Verse 3:
It's a cool place and they say it gets colder.
You're bundled up now, wait till you get older.
But the meteor men beg to differ,
Judging by the hole in the satellite picture.
The ice we skate is getting pretty thin.
The water's getting warm, so you might as well swim.
My world's on fire, how about yours?
That's the way I like it and I'll never get bored.
(To Chorus:)

Verse 4:
Somebody once asked, could I spare some change for gas.
I need to get myself away from this place.
I said, "Yep, what a concept;
I could use a little fuel myself
And we could all use a little change."
(To Verse 5:)

From the LUCASFILM LTD. Production "STAR WARS: Episode I The Phantom Menace"

ANAKIN'S THEME

By JOHN WILLIAMS
Arranged by DAN COATES

Moderately slow

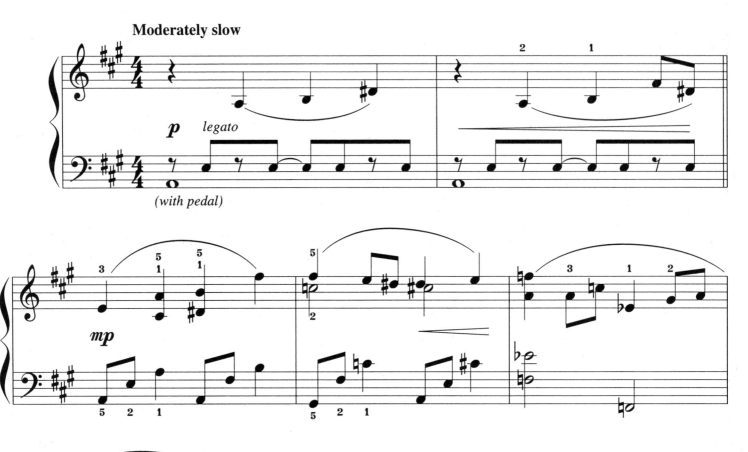

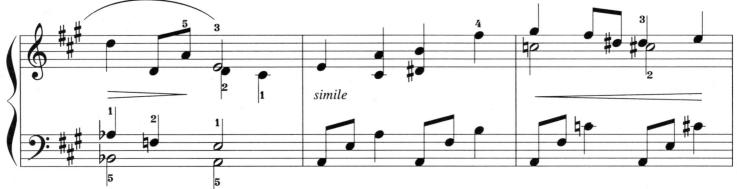

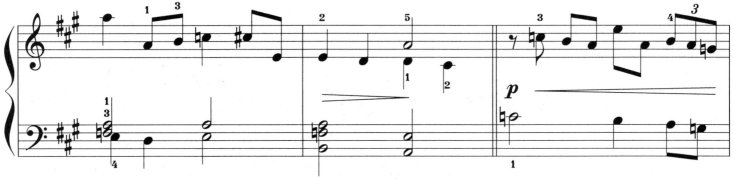

Anakin's Theme - 3 - 1

Anakin's Theme - 3 - 2

From the Fox 2000 Motion Picture "ANYWHERE BUT HERE"

ANYWHERE BUT HERE

Words and Music by
k.d. lang and RICK NOWELS

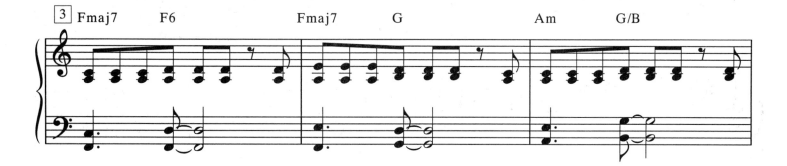

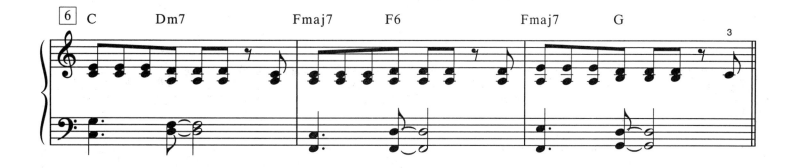

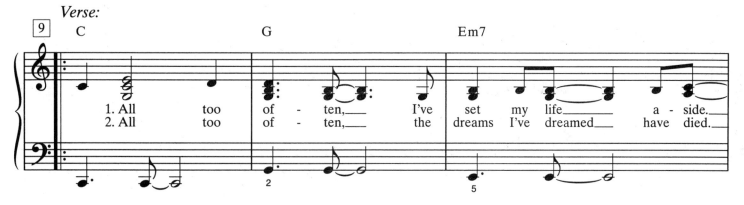

1. All too of - ten,___ I've set my life_____ a - side.___
2. All too of - ten,___ the dreams I've dreamed_____ have died.___

Anywhere But Here - 5 - 1

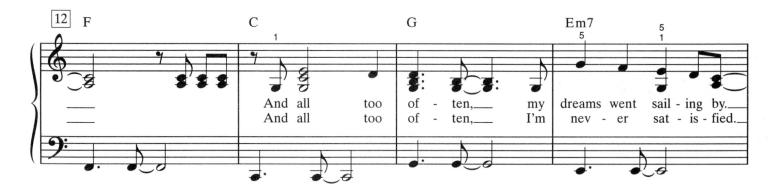

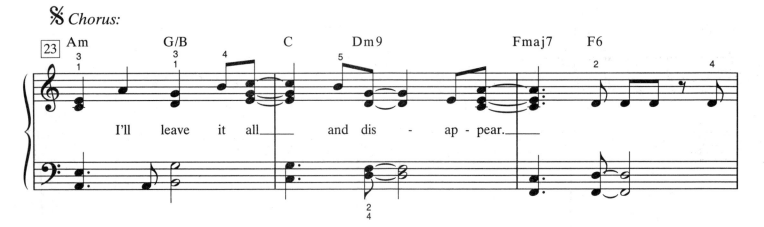

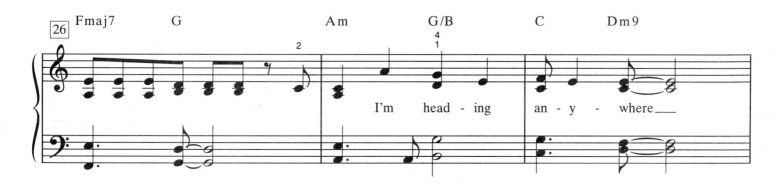

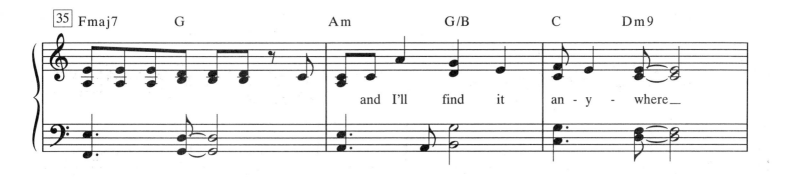

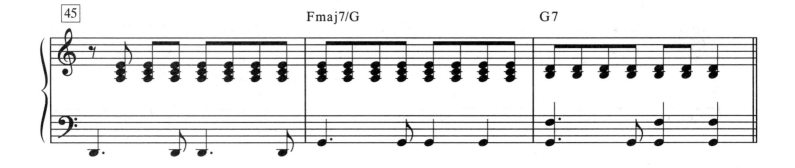

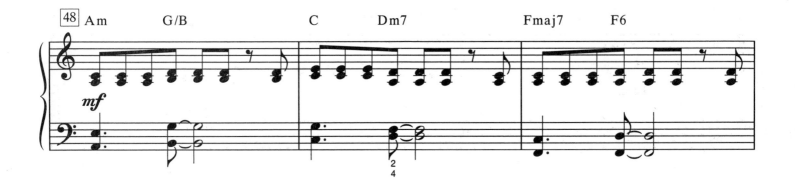

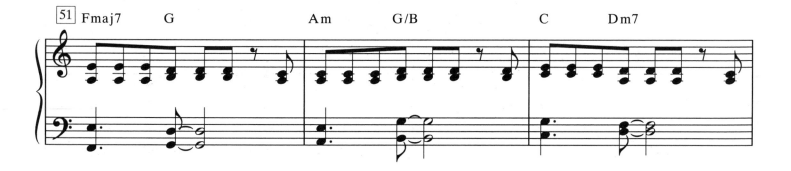

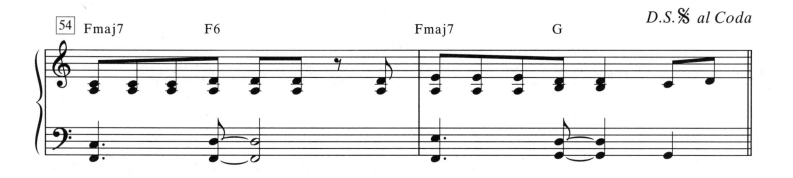

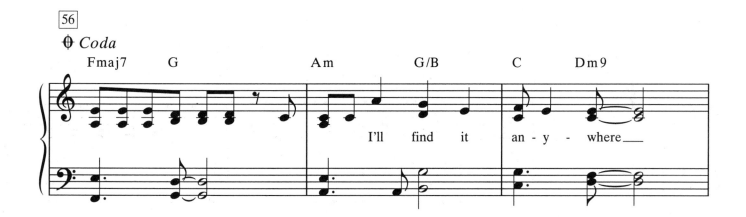

I'll find it an-y-where___

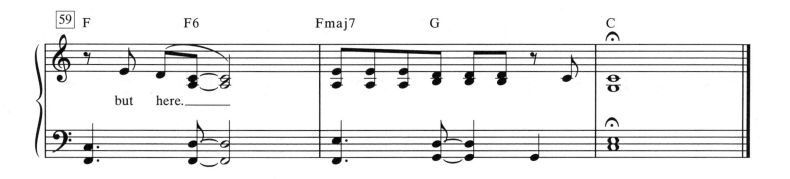

but here._____

WHEN I SAID I DO

Words and Music by
CLINT BLACK
Arranged by DAN COATES

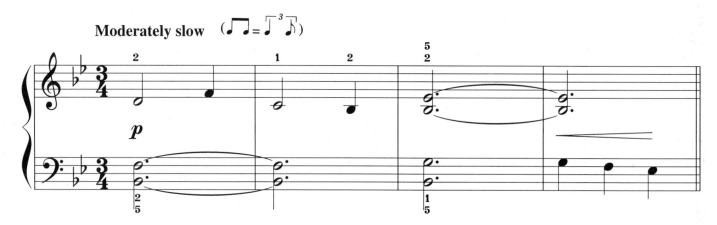

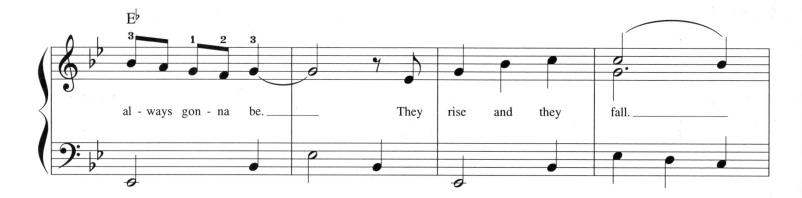

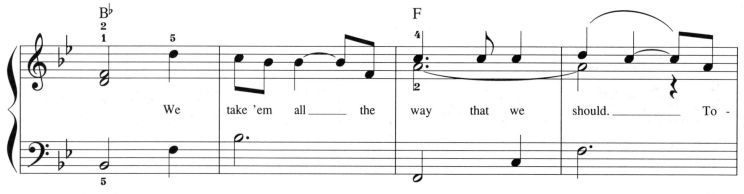

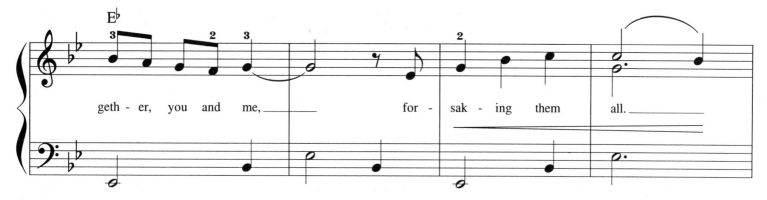

geth - er, you and me, _____ for - sak - ing them all. _____

Deep in the night ___ and by the light ___ of day, _____ it

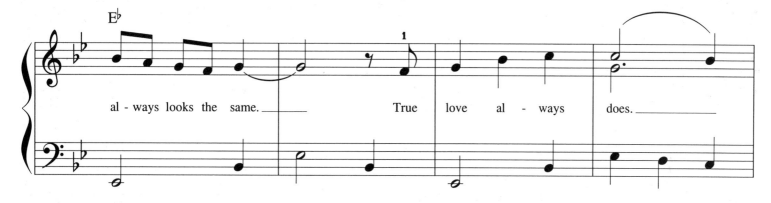

al - ways looks the same. _____ True love al - ways does. _____

And here by your side, we're a mil - lion miles a - way. ___ Noth - ing's

ev - er gon - na change the way I feel. The way it is is the way that it

Chorus:

was. ___ When I said I do, I meant that I will, ___

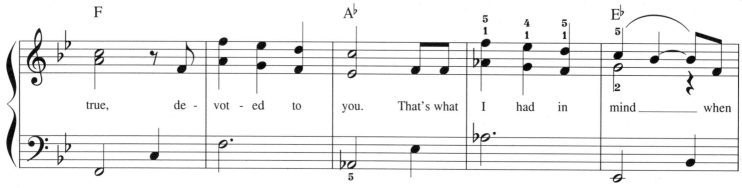

___ 'til the end of all time, be faith - ful and

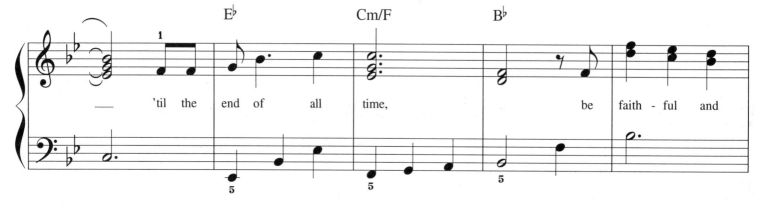

true, de - vot - ed to you. That's what I had in mind ___ when

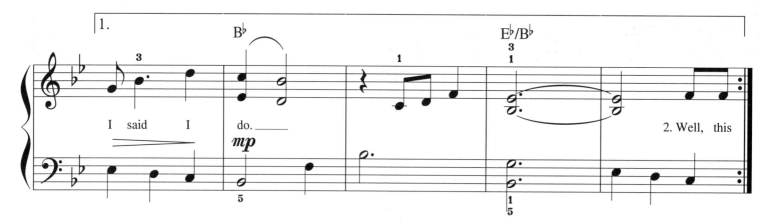

1.

I said I do. ___ 2. Well, this

2.

I said I do. ___ Tru - er than true, you

BAILAMOS

Words and Music by
PAUL BARRY and MARK TAYLOR
Arranged by DAN COATES

Bailamos - 5 - 1

world in ___ out - side; ___ don't let a mo - ment ___ go by.
leav - ing ___ your side; ___ we're gon - na dance through ___ the night.

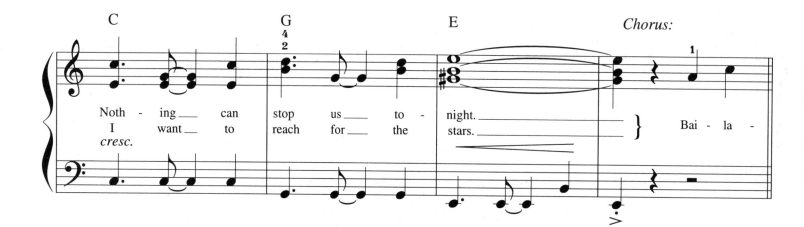

Noth - ing ___ can stop us ___ to - night. ___ Bai - la -
I want ___ to reach for ___ the stars. ___
cresc.

Chorus:

mos, ___ let the rhy - thm take ___ you o - ver, bai - la -
f

mos. ___ Te quie - ro, a - mor mi - o, bai - la -

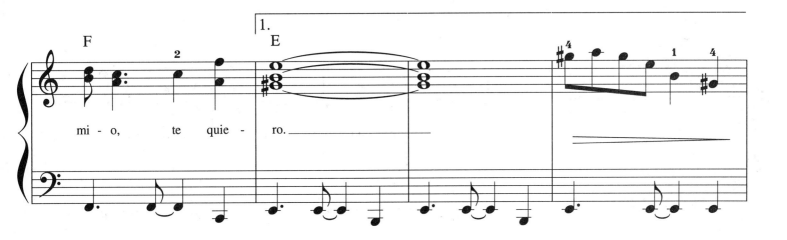

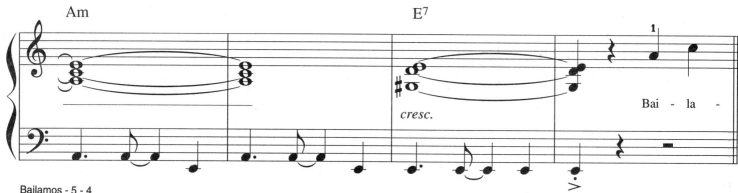

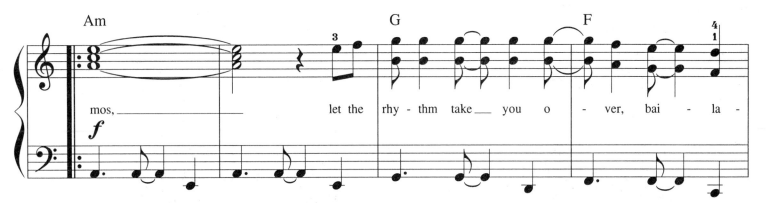

Bailamos - 5 - 5

...BABY ONE MORE TIME

Words and Music by
MAX MARTIN
Arranged by DAN COATES

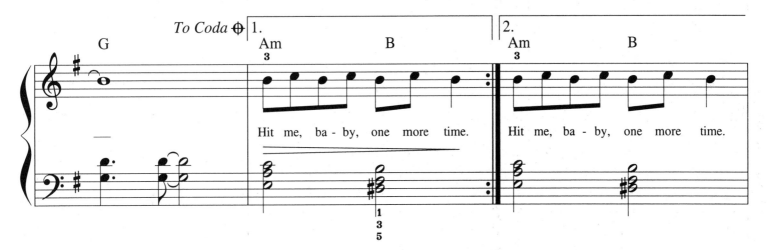

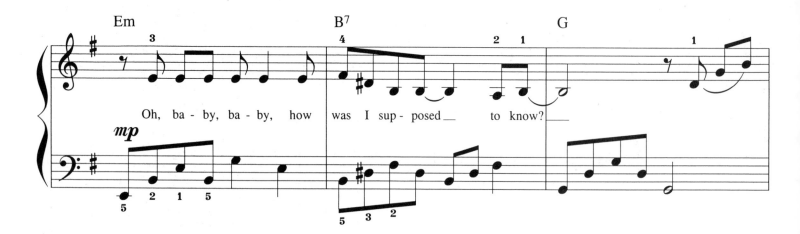

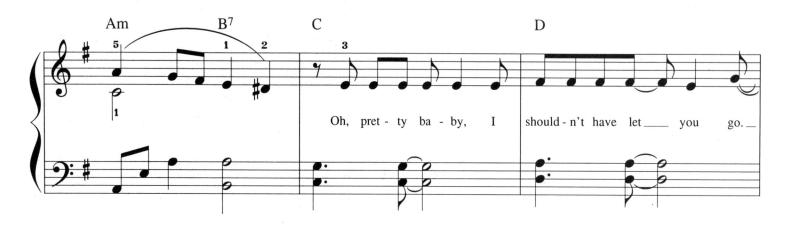

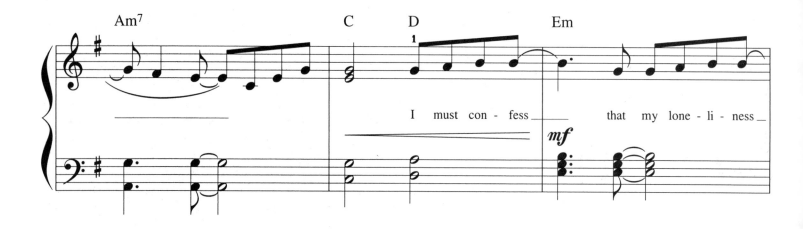

D.S. 𝄋 al Coda

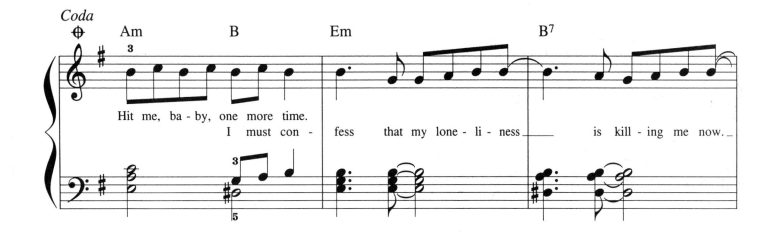

that you will be here ___ and give me a sign. ___ Hit me, ba - by, one more time.

Coda

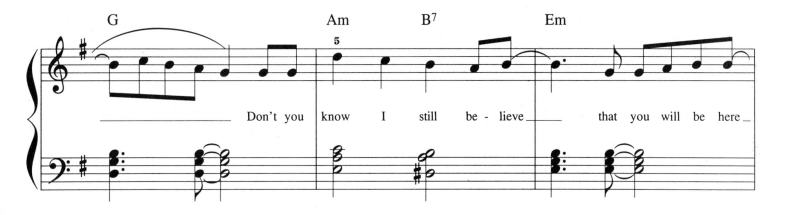

Hit me, ba - by, one more time. I must con - fess that my lone - li - ness ___ is kill - ing me now. ___

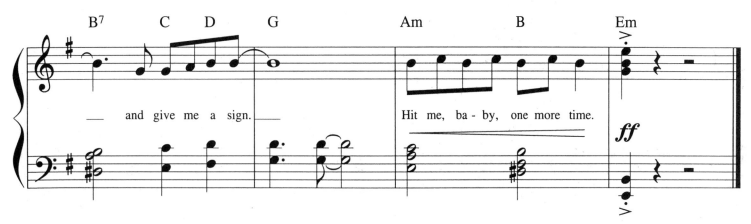

___ Don't you know I still be - lieve ___ that you will be here ___

___ and give me a sign. ___ Hit me, ba - by, one more time.

BACK AT ONE

Words and Music by
BRIAN McKNIGHT
Arranged by DAN COATES

Back at One - 4 - 1

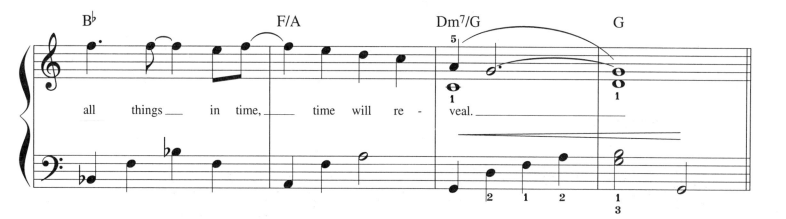

all things ___ in time, ___ time will re - veal. ___

Chorus:

One, you're like a dream come true. Two, just wan - na be with you.

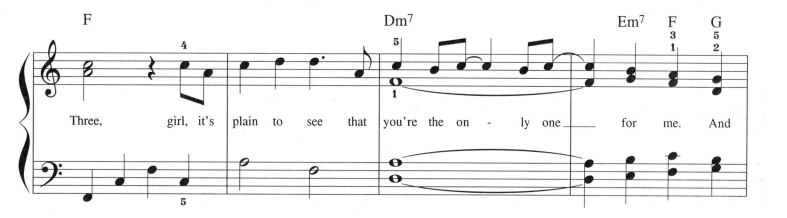

Three, girl, it's plain to see that you're the on - ly one ___ for me. And

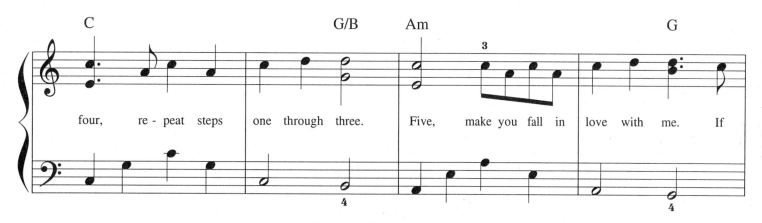

four, re - peat steps one through three. Five, make you fall in love with me. If

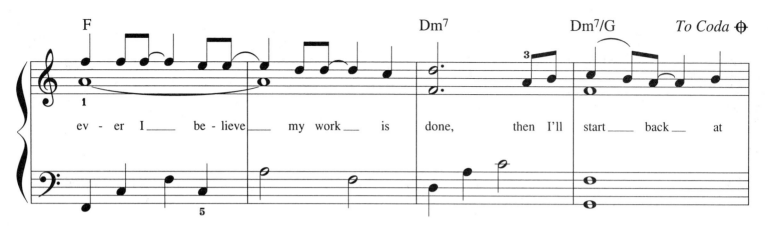

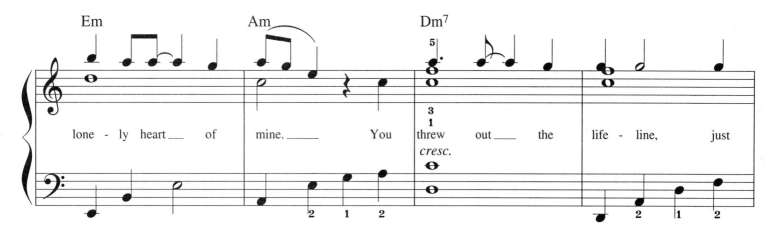

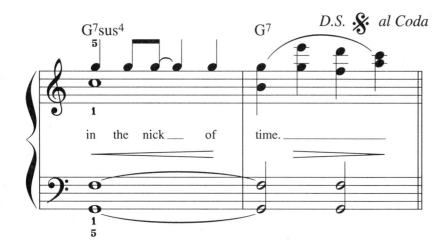

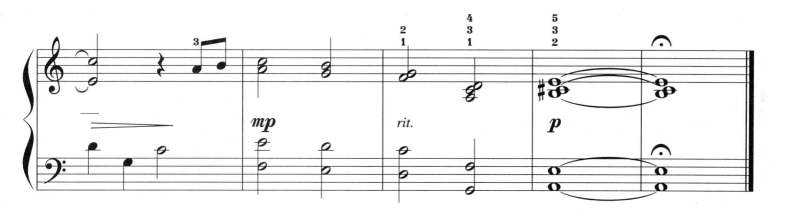

Lyrics:

lone - ly heart ___ of mine. ___ You threw out ___ the life - line, just in the nick ___ of time. ___ one.

Verse 2:
It's so incredible,
The way things work themselves out.
And all emotional
Once you know what it's all about.
And undesirable
For us to be apart.
I never would have made it very far,
'Cause you know you've got the keys to my heart.
(To Chorus:)

From the Motion Picture AUSTIN POWERS: The Spy Who Shagged Me

BEAUTIFUL STRANGER

Words and Music by
MADONNA CICCONE and WILLIAM ORBIT
Arranged by DAN COATES

Beautiful Stranger - 5 - 1

I'll take my chance on a beau - ti - ful strang - er.

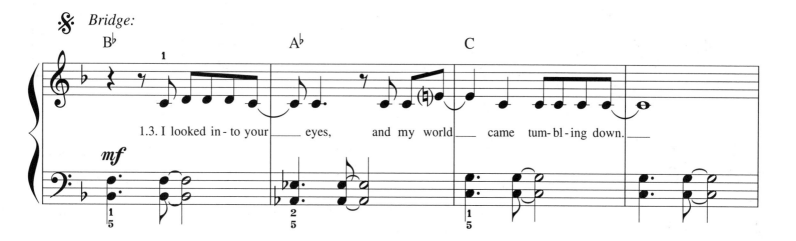

𝄋 *Bridge:*

1.3. I looked in - to your eyes, and my world came tum - bl - ing down.

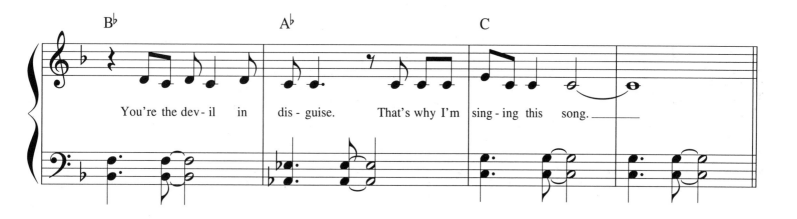

You're the dev - il in dis - guise. That's why I'm sing - ing this song.

Chorus:

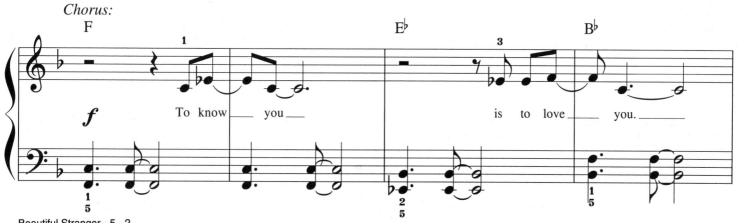

To know you is to love you.

44

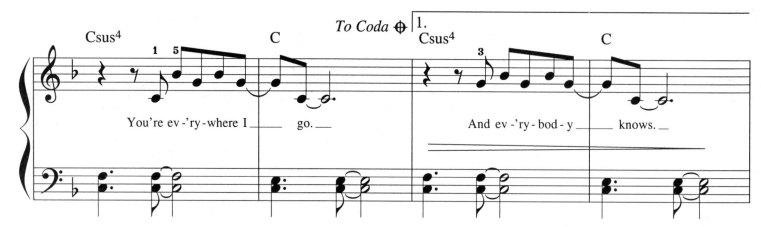

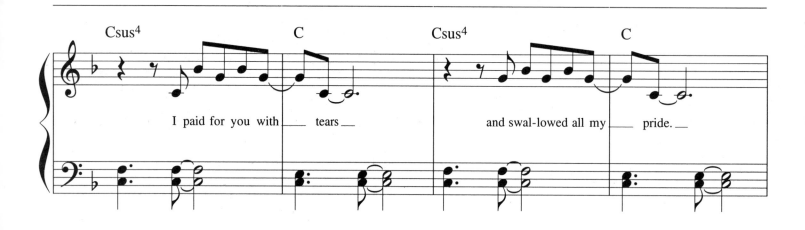

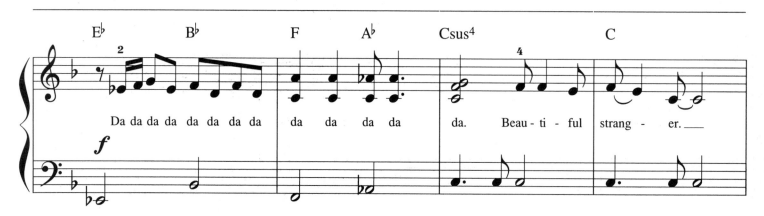

Beautiful Stranger - 5 - 3

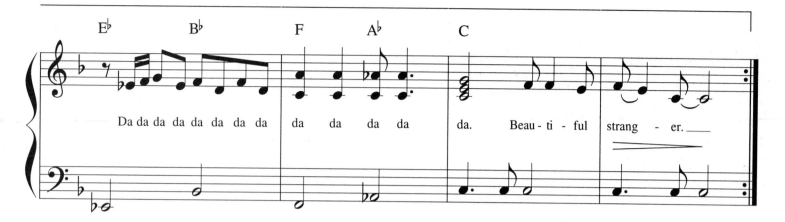

Da da da da da da da da da da da da da. Beau-ti-ful strang - er.___

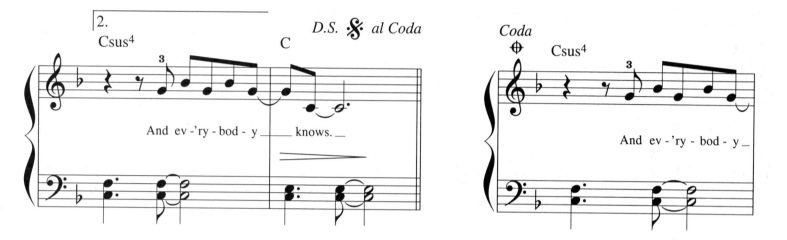

2.
Csus⁴   C
And ev-'ry-bod-y ___ knows. ___

D.S. 𝄋 al Coda

Coda
Csus⁴
And ev-'ry-bod-y ___

C   Csus⁴   C   Csus⁴
___ knows. ___   I paid for you with ___ tears ___   and swal-lowed all my ___

C   B♭   F   A♭
___ pride. ___   Da da da da da da da da da da da da

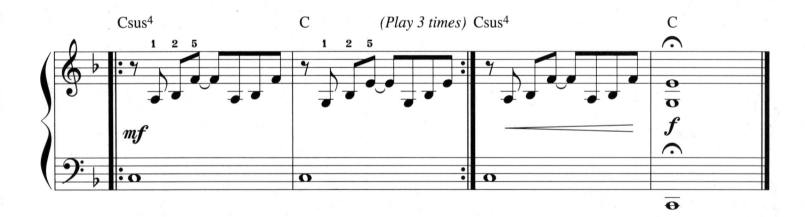

Verse 3:
If I'm smart, then I'll run away.
But I'm not, so I guess I'll stay.
Haven't you heard?
I fell in love with a beautiful stranger.

Bridge 2:
I looked into your face,
My heart was dancin' all over the place.
I'd like to change my point of view,
If I could just forget about you.
(To Chorus:)

BELIEVE

Words and Music by
BRIAN HIGGINS, STUART McLENNAN, PAUL BARRY,
STEPHEN TORCH, MATT GRAY and TIM POWELL
Arranged by DAN COATES

Believe - 3 - 1

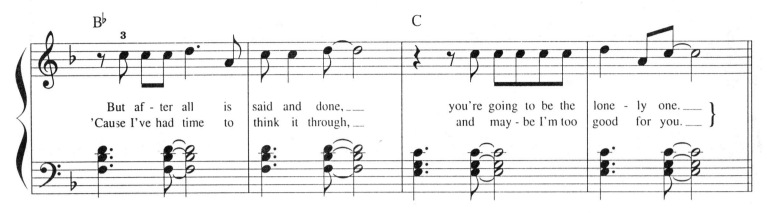

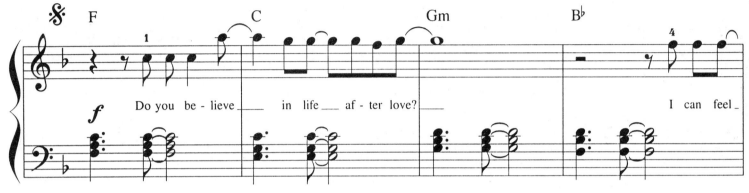

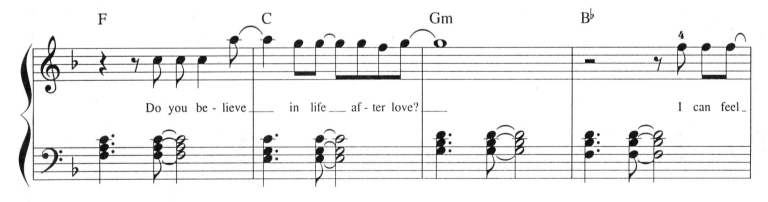

Last time, to Coda

But I know ___ that I'll ___ get through ___ this, ___

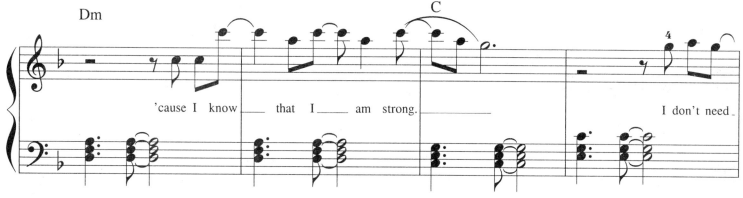

'cause I know ___ that I ___ am strong. ___ I don't need ___

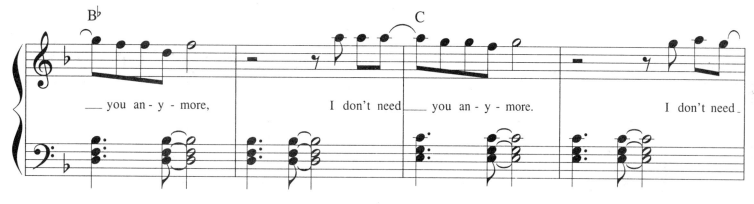

___ you an - y - more, I don't need ___ you an - y - more. I don't need ___

D.S. 𝄋 al Coda

___ you a - ny - more, no, I don't need you an - y - more.

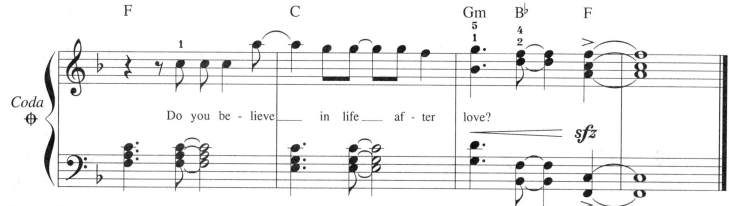

Coda

Do you be - lieve ___ in life ___ af - ter love?

Believe - 3 - 3

(YOU DRIVE ME) CRAZY

Words and Music by JORGEN ELOFSSON,
DAVID KREUGER, PER MAGNUSSON and
MAX MARTIN
Arranged by DAN COATES

Moderate dance beat ♩ = 92

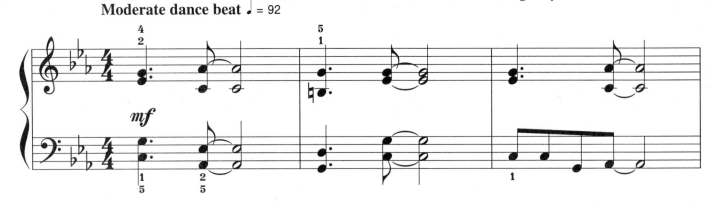

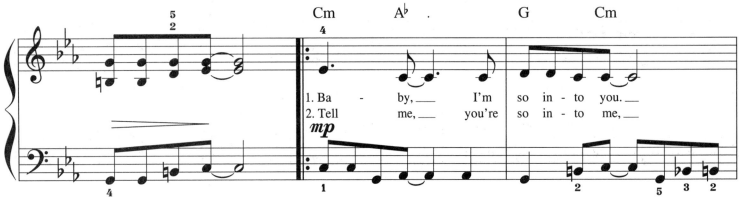

1st time only

Ev - 'ry time you look at me, ___ my heart is jump - ing. It's

eas - y to see. ___ Lov - in' you means so much more, ___

more than an - y - thing I ev - er felt be - fore. __ You drive me cra - zy, ___ I

just can't sleep. ___ I'm so ex - cit - ed, I'm in too deep. __ You drive me

To Coda ⊕

cra - zy, ___ but it feels al - right. ___ Ba - by, think - in' of you keeps me

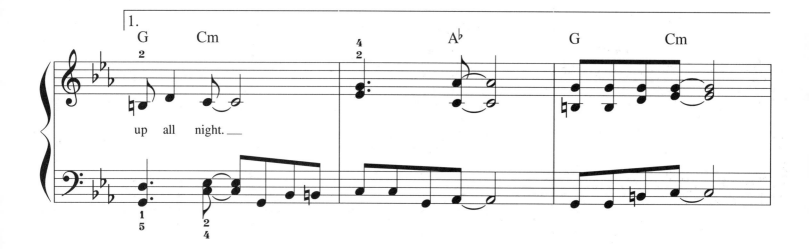

up all night. ___

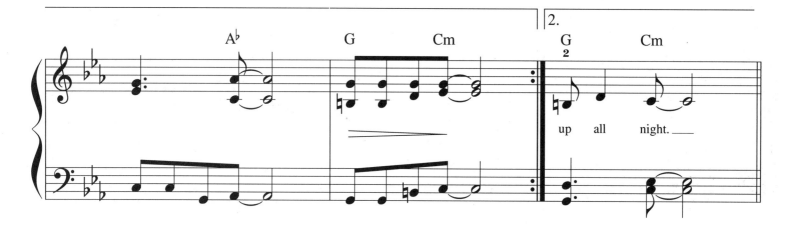

up all night. ___

Cra - zy, ___ I just can't sleep. ___ I'm so ex - cit - ed, I'm

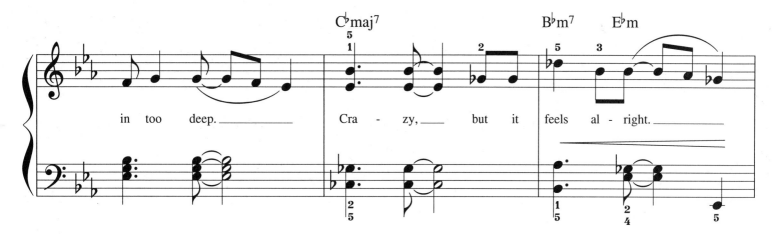

in too deep._____ Cra - zy,___ but it feels al - right._____

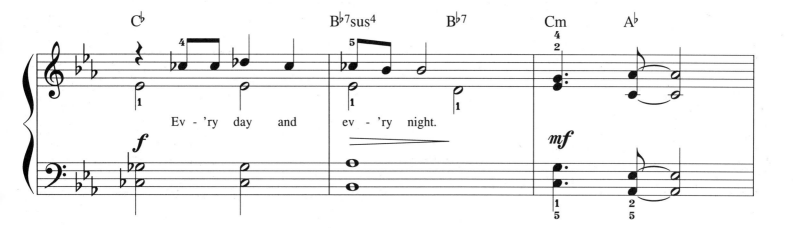

Ev - 'ry day and ev - 'ry night.

D.S. 𝄋 *al Coda*

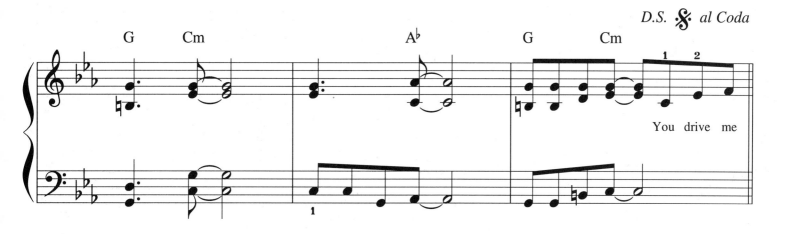

You drive me

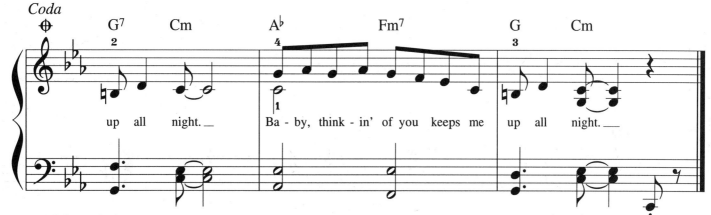

Coda

up all night.__ Ba - by, think - in' of you keeps me up all night.__

(You Drive Me) Crazy - 4 - 4

C'EST LA VIE

Arranged by
JOHN BRIMHALL

Words and Music by
B*WITCHED, HEDGES BRANNIGAN
and ACKERMAN

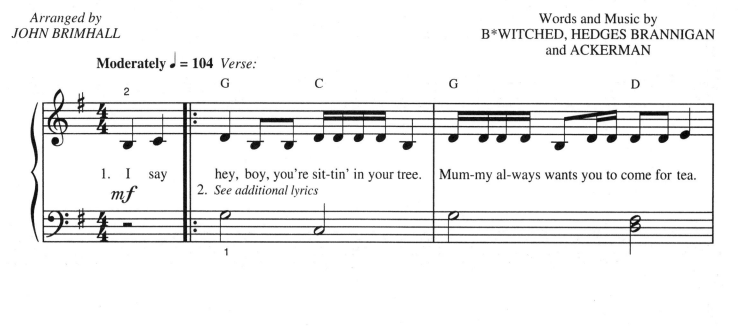

1. I say hey, boy, you're sit-tin' in your tree.
2. *See additional lyrics*

Mum-my al-ways wants you to come for tea.

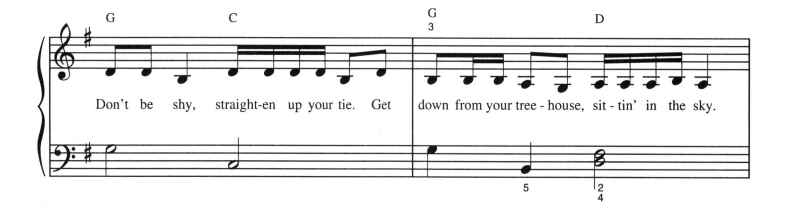

Don't be shy, straight-en up your tie. Get down from your tree - house, sit - tin' in the sky.

I wan-na know just what to do. Is it ver - y big? Is there room for two?

I got a house with__ win-dows and doors. I'll show you mine if you'll show me yours.__

Pre-chorus:

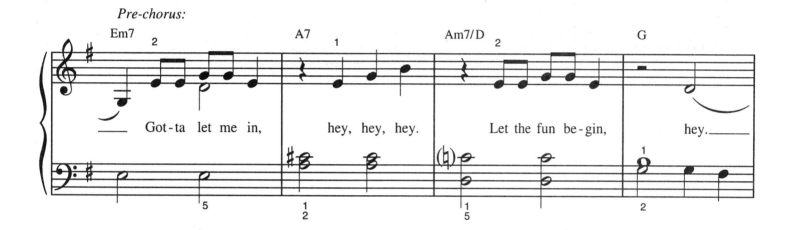

__ Got-ta let me in, hey, hey, hey. Let the fun be-gin, hey.__

__ I'm the wolf to-day, hey, hey, hey. I'll huff, I'll puff, I'll

Chorus:

huff, I'll puff, I'll blow you a - way.__
Say you will,__ } say you won't. Say you'll do what I don't. Say you're

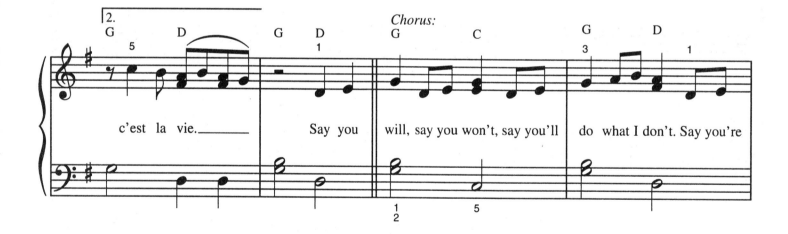

do what I don't. Say you're true, say to me, c'est la vie.

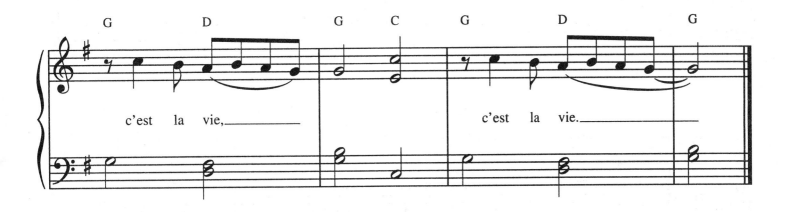

c'est la vie, c'est la vie.

Verse 2:
Do you play with the girls, play with the boys?
Do you ever get lonely playing with your toys?
We can talk, we can sing.
I'll be the queen and you'll be the king.
Hey, boy, in your tree,
Throw down your ladder, make room for me.
(To Pre-chorus:)

DOWN SO LONG

Arranged by
JOHN BRIMHALL

Words and Music by
JEWEL KILCHER

Moderately slow ♩ = 76

Verse 1:

Sun - sets 'cross the o - cean._ I'm a thou-sand miles_ from_

an - y - where. My pock - et - book and my heart both just got

sto - len, and that sun acts like she don't e - ven care._

Verses 2 & 3:

2. The wind blows cold_ when you reach_ the top. It feels like
3. *See additional lyrics*

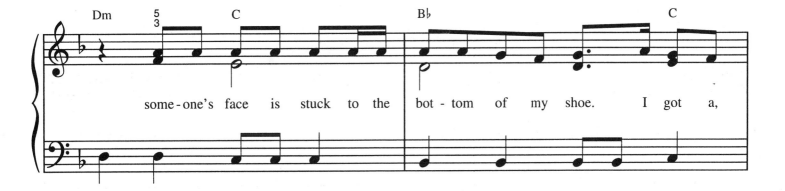

some-one's face is stuck to the bot-tom of my shoe. I got a,

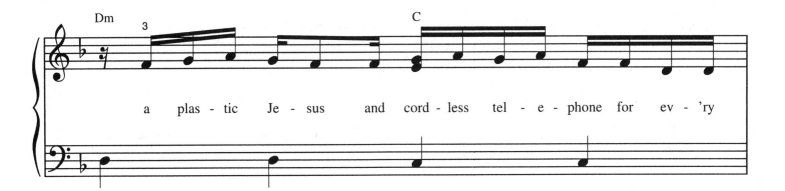

a plas-tic Je-sus and cord-less tel-e-phone for ev-'ry

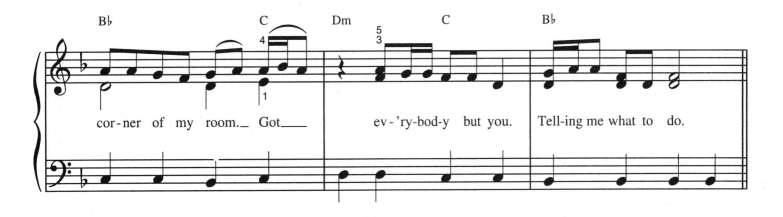

cor-ner of my room.__ Got__ ev-'ry-bod-y but you. Tell-ing me what to do.

Chorus:

But I've been down__ so long,_____ ooh, it can't be long-er

To Coda ⊕

still._____ I've been down_ so long_____ that the

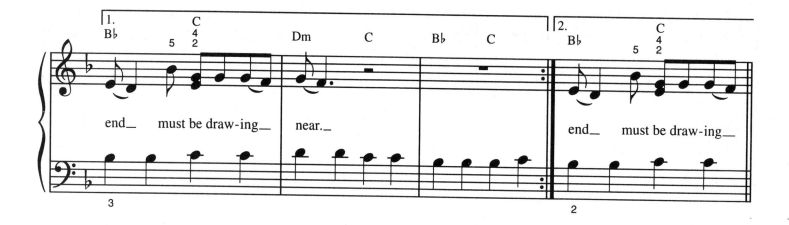

end_ must be draw-ing_ near._ end_ must be draw-ing_

near,_ ee oh ee oh. Oh_____ ee oh ee oh. Oh_____ ee oh ee oh, oh._

____ I take a trip, I catch a train, I catch a plane, I got a

 tick - et in my___ hand,___ and then a fat man takes my mon - ey and like

D.S. 𝄋 al Coda

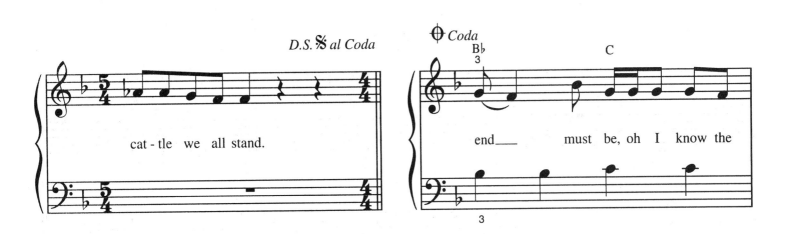

cat - tle we all stand.

Coda

end___ must be, oh I know the

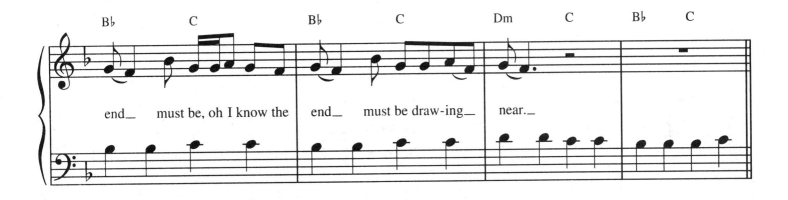

end__ must be, oh I know the end__ must be draw-ing__ near.__

Repeat ad lib. and fade

Oh___ ee oh ee oh. Oh___ ee oh ee oh. Oh__ ee oh ee oh, oh._____

Verse 3:
I look to everybody but me to answer my prayers,
Till I saw an angel in a bathroom who said she saw no one worth saving anywhere.
And a blind man on the corner said it's simple, like flipping a coin:
Don't matter what side it lands on if it's someone else's dime.
(To Chorus:)

DUEL OF THE FATES

By JOHN WILLIAMS
Arranged by Dan Coates

Maestoso, with great force

Kor - ah, _____ Mah - tah. _____ Kor - ah, _____ Rah - tah - mah.

Allegro ♩ = 152

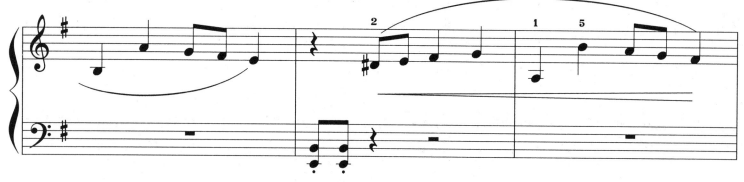

1.

2.

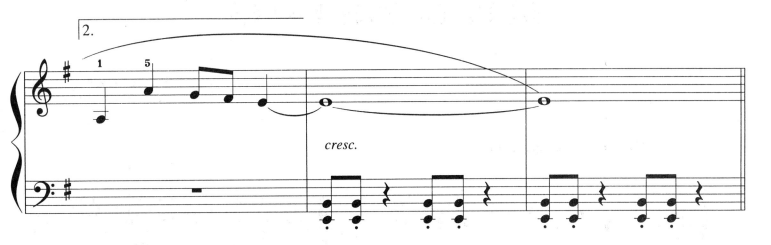

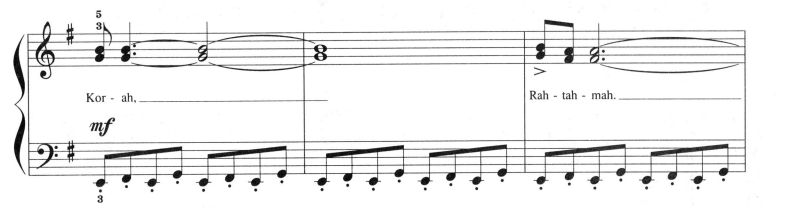

Kor - ah,

Rah - tah - mah.

Yood - hah,

Kor - ah.

64

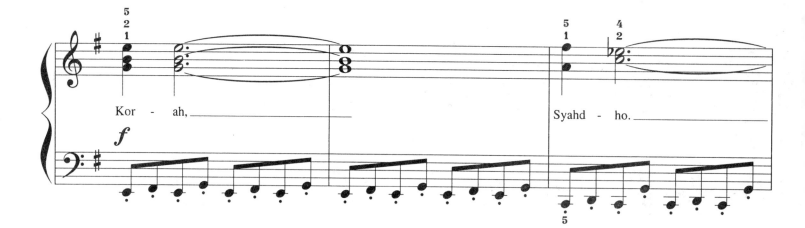

Kor - ah,_____ Syahd - ho._____

Rah - tah - mah,_____

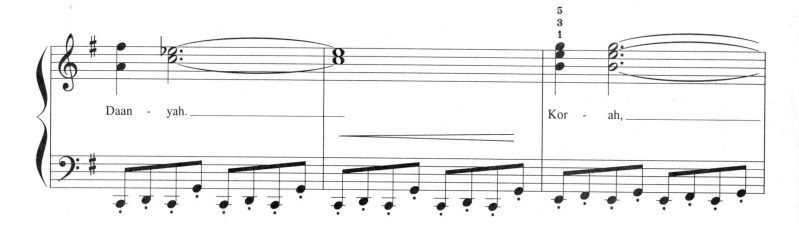

Daan - yah._____ Kor - ah,_____

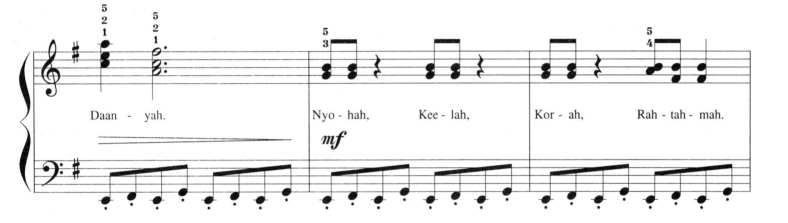

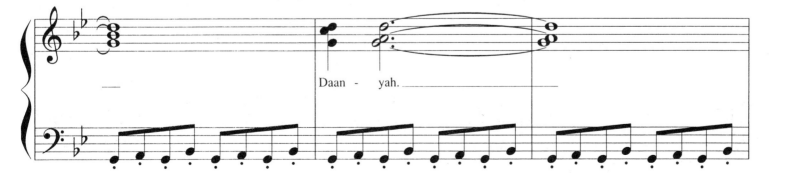

Kor - ah, _____ Rah - tah - mah. _____

mp

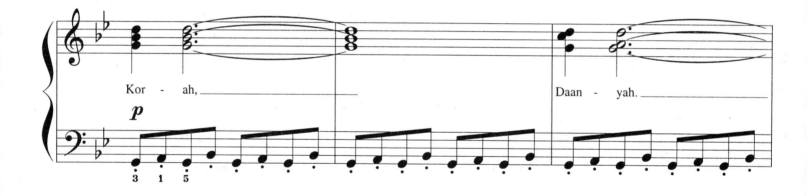

Kor - ah, _____ Daan - yah. _____

p

Kor - ah, _____

mf

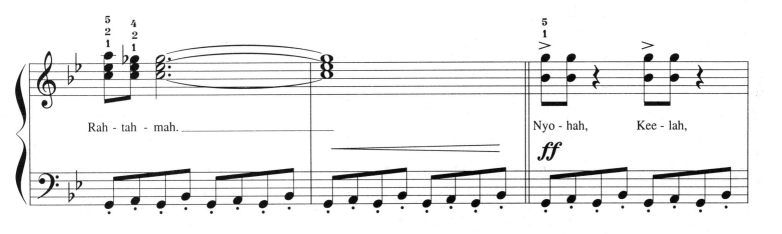

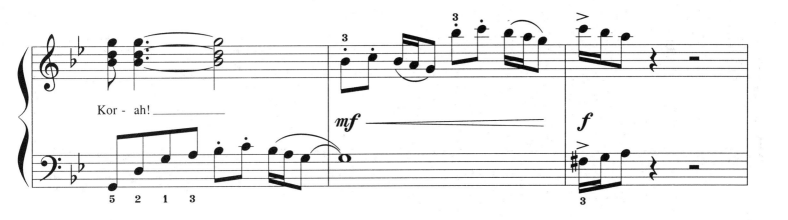

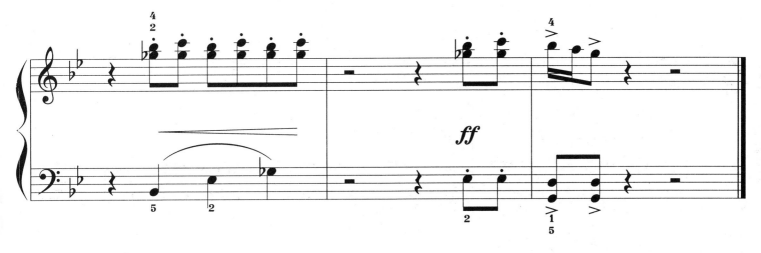

FROM THIS MOMENT ON

Words and Music by
SHANIA TWAIN and R.J. LANGE
Arranged by DAN COATES

From This Moment On - 3 - 1

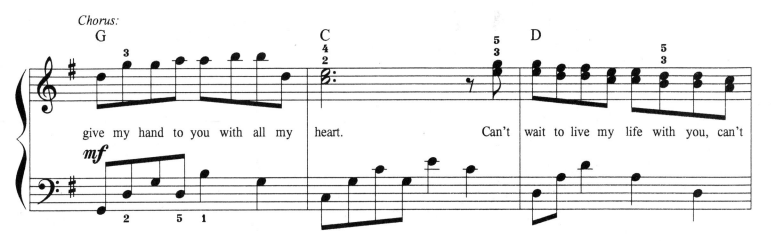

Chorus:

give my hand to you with all my heart. Can't wait to live my life with you, can't

wait to start. You and I will nev - er be a - part. My

To Coda ⊕ *D.S.* 𝄋 *al Coda*

dreams came true be - cause of you.____ 3. From this

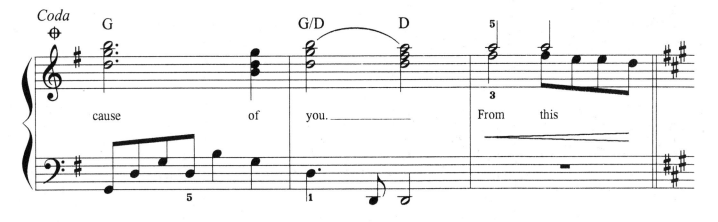

Coda ⊕

cause of you.____ From this

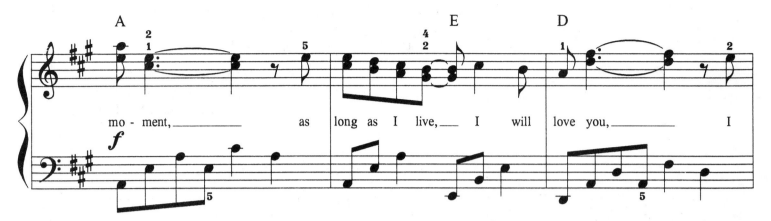

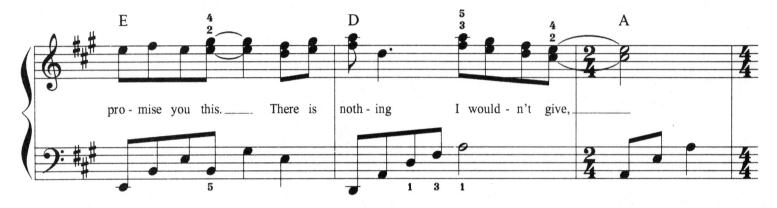

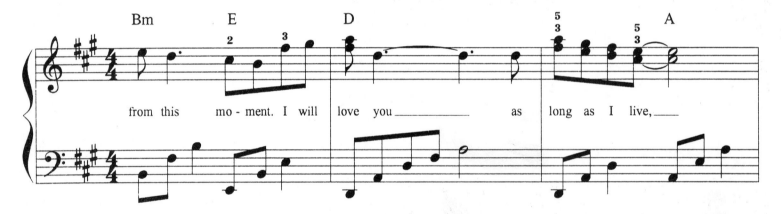

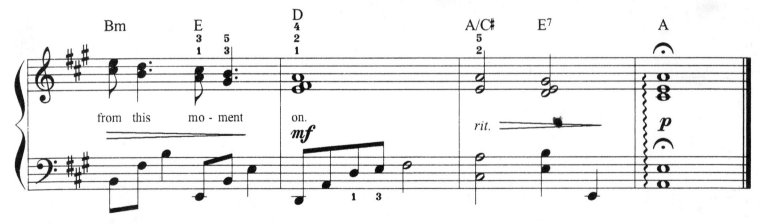

Verse 3:
From this moment, as long as I live,
I will love you, I promise you this.
There is nothing I wouldn't give,
From this moment on.

Chorus 2:
You're the reason I believe in love.
And you're the answer to my prayers from up above.
All we need is just the two of us.
My dreams came true
Because of you.

From the Fox Searchlight Film, "THE BROTHERS McMULLEN"

I WILL REMEMBER YOU

Words and Music by
SARAH McLACHLAN, SEAMUS EGAN
and DAVID MERENDA
Arranged by DAN COATES

Slowly

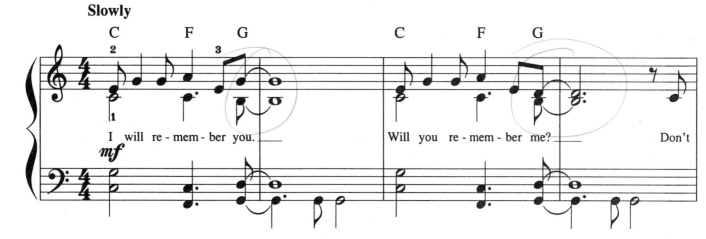

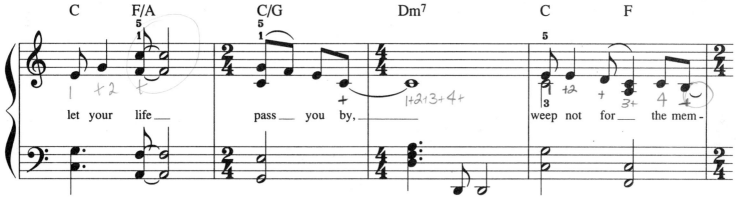

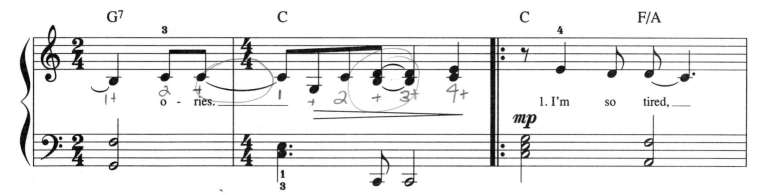

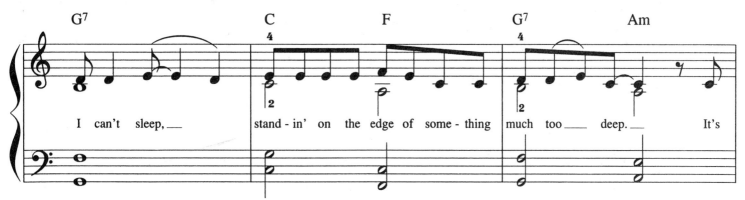

I Will Remember You - 3 - 1

72

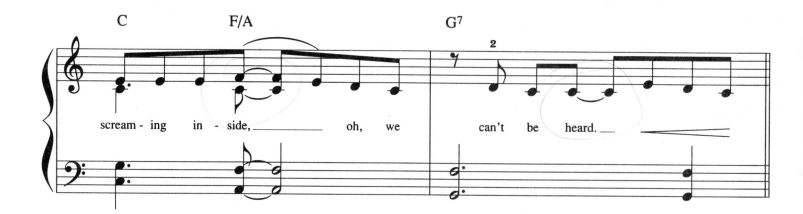

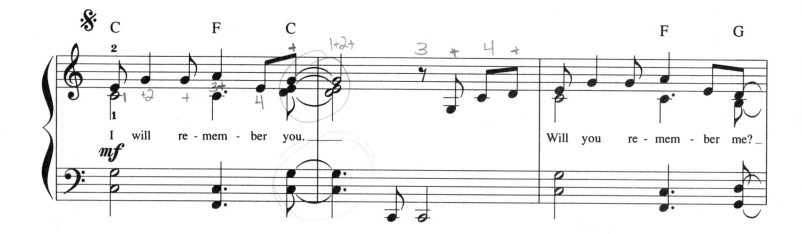

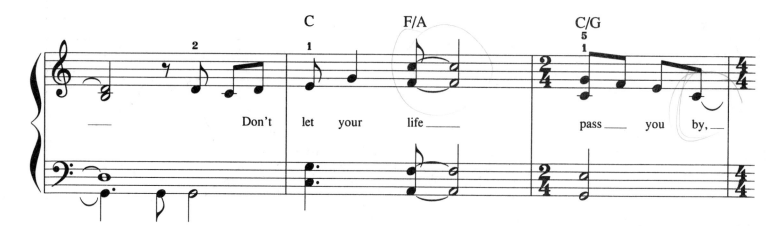

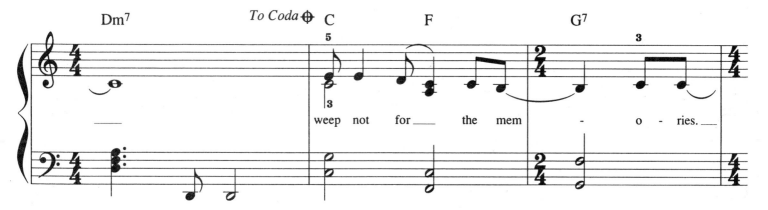

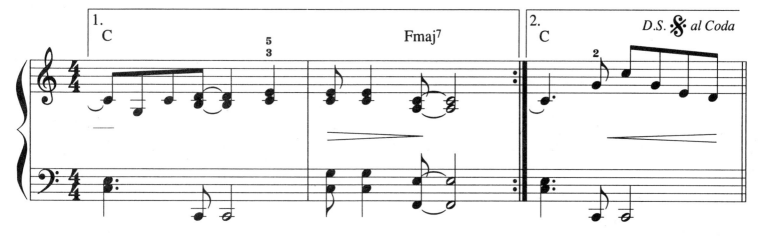

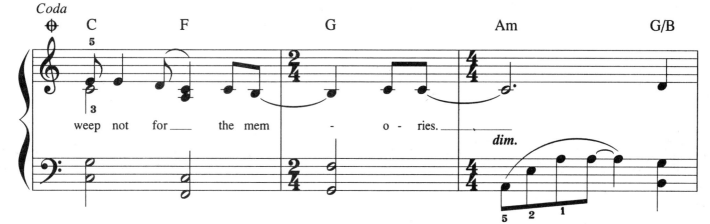

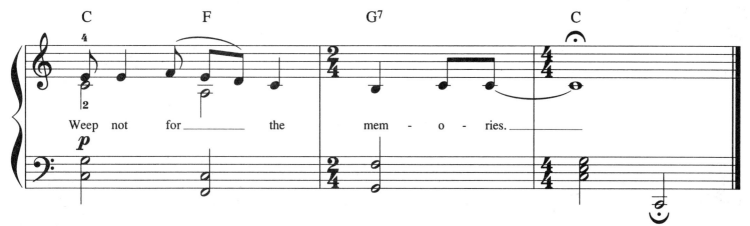

Verse 2:
So afraid to love you, more afraid to lose.
I'm clinging to a past that doesn't let me choose.
Where once there was a darkness, a deep and endless night,
You gave me everything you had, oh, you gave me life.
(To Chorus:)

I Will Remember You - 3 - 3

GENIE IN A BOTTLE

Words and Music by
PAMELA SHEYNE, DAVID FRANK
and STEVE KIPNER
Arranged by DAN COATES

Moderately slow ♩ = 84

feel like I've __ been locked up tight for a cen - tu - ry __ of lone - ly nights,
Mu - sic's play - ing and the light's down low. Just one more dance and then we're good to go.

wait - ing for some - one _____ to re - lease me. You're
Wait - ing for some - one _____ who __ needs me.

Genie in a Bottle - 4 - 1

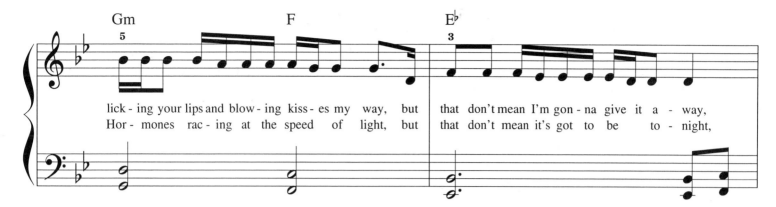

lick - ing your lips and blow - ing kiss - es my way, but that don't mean I'm gon - na give it a - way,
Hor - mones rac - ing at the speed of light, but that don't mean it's got to be to - night,

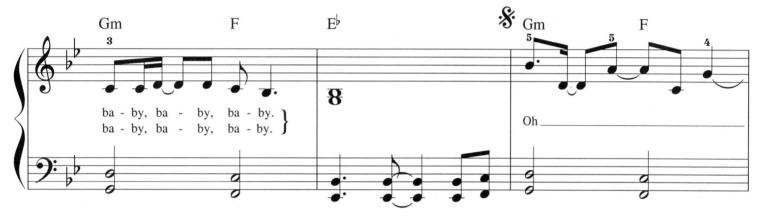

ba - by, ba - by, ba - by.
ba - by, ba - by, ba - by.

Oh _____

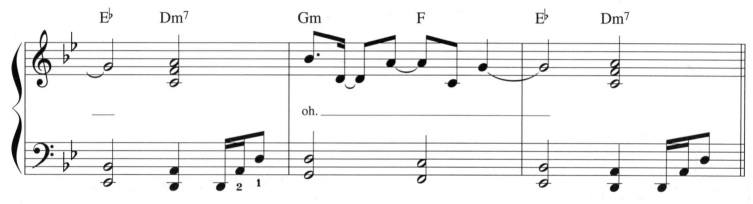

_____ oh.

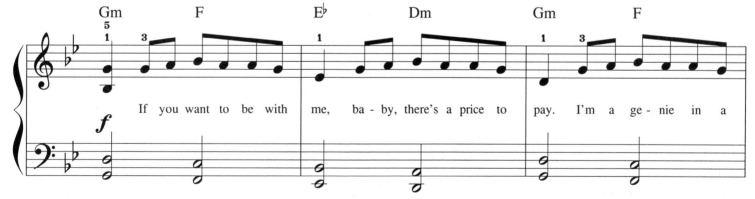

If you want to be with me, ba - by, there's a price to pay. I'm a ge - nie in a

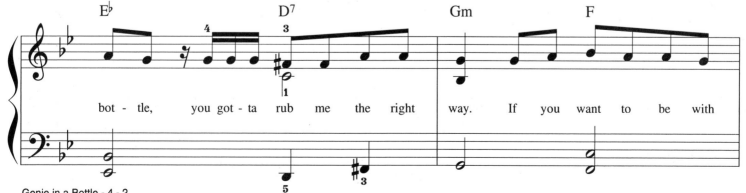

bot - tle, you got - ta rub me the right way. If you want to be with

D.S. ⅜ al Coda

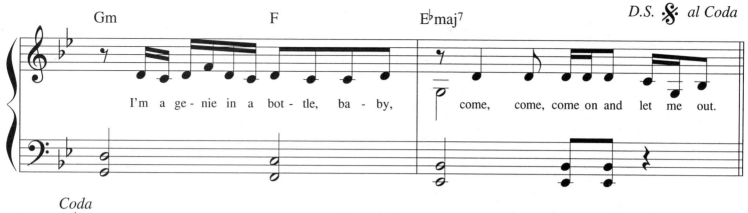

I'm a ge-nie in a bot-tle, ba-by, come, come, come on and let me out.

Coda

If you want to be with me, ba-by, there's a price to pay. I'm a ge-nie in a

bot-tle, you got-ta rub me the right way. If you want to be with

me, I can make your wish come true. Just come and set me free,__ ba-by, and I'll be with you.

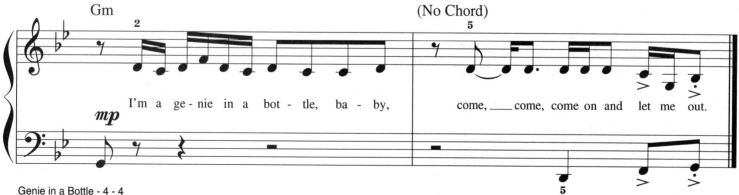

I'm a ge-nie in a bot-tle, ba-by, come,__ come, come on and let me out.

I DO (CHERISH YOU)

Words and Music by
KEITH STEGALL and DAN HILL
Arranged by DAN COATES

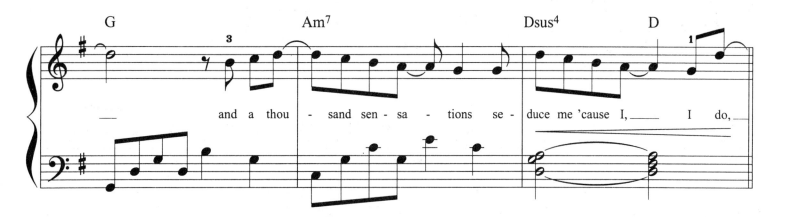

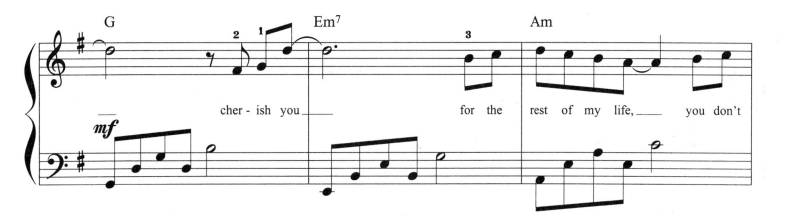

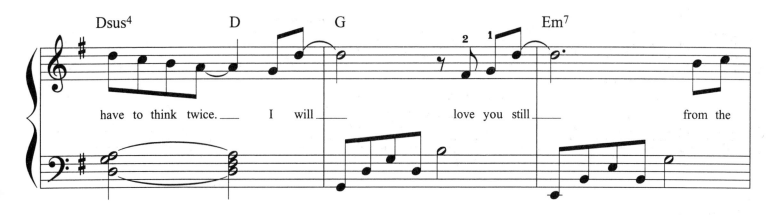

80

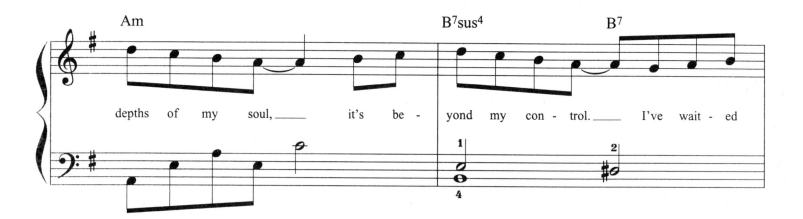

depths of my soul, _____ it's be - yond my con - trol. _____ I've wait - ed

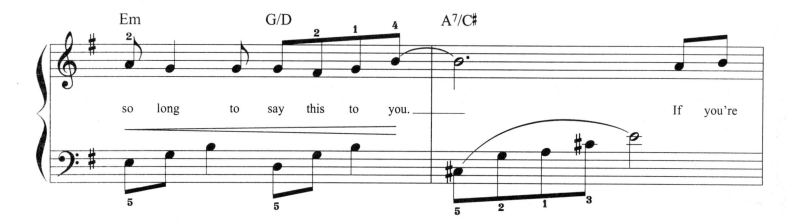

so long to say this to you. _____ If you're

ask - ing do I love you this much, _____ I do.

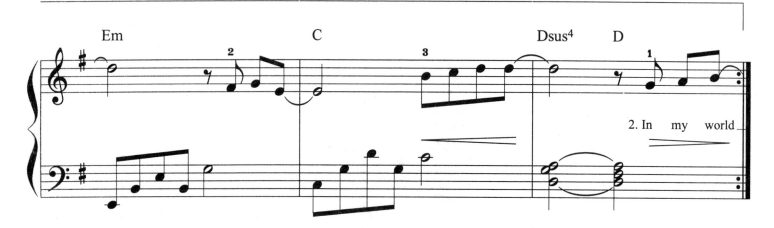

2. In my world

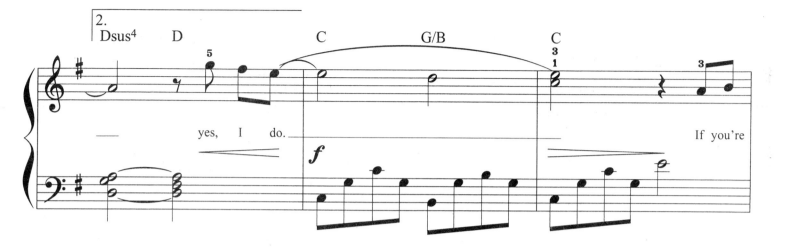

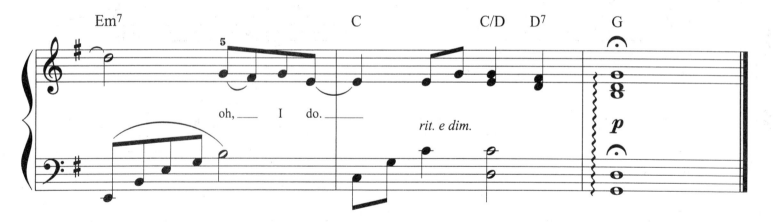

Verse 2:
In my world before you,
I lived outside my emotions.
Didn't know where I was going
Till that day I found you.
How you opened my life
To a new paradise.

In a world torn by change,
Still, with all of my heart
Till my dying day,
I do cherish you.   *(To Chorus:)*

From Touchstone Pictures' ''ARMAGEDDON''

I DON'T WANT TO MISS A THING

Words and Music by
DIANE WARREN
Arranged by DAN COATES

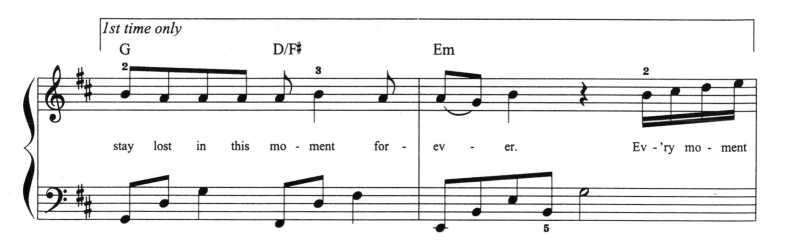

stay lost in this mo - ment for - ev - er. Ev -'ry mo - ment

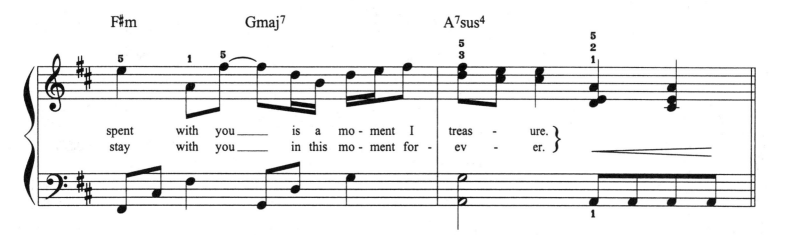

spent with you____ is a mo - ment I treas - ure.
stay with you____ in this mo - ment for - ev - er. }

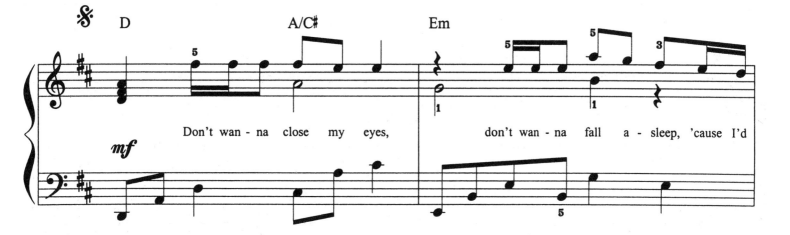

Don't wan - na close my eyes, don't wan - na fall a - sleep, 'cause I'd

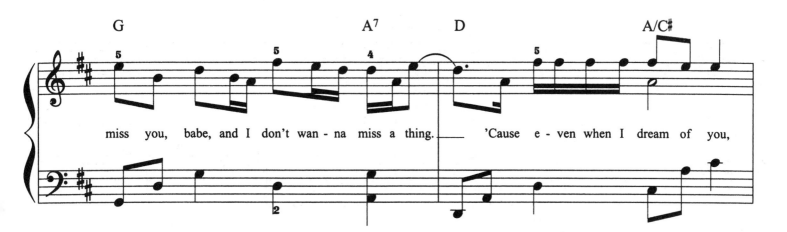

miss you, babe, and I don't wan - na miss a thing.____ 'Cause e - ven when I dream of you,

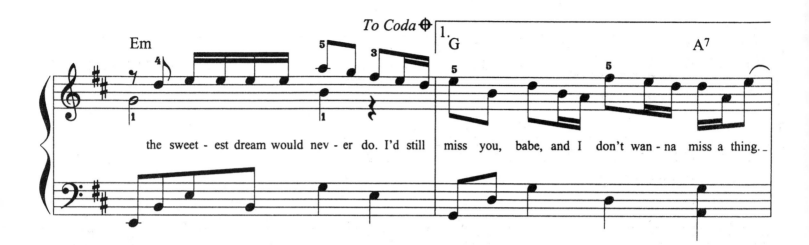

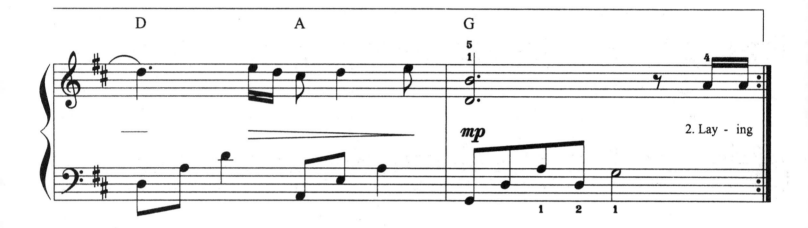

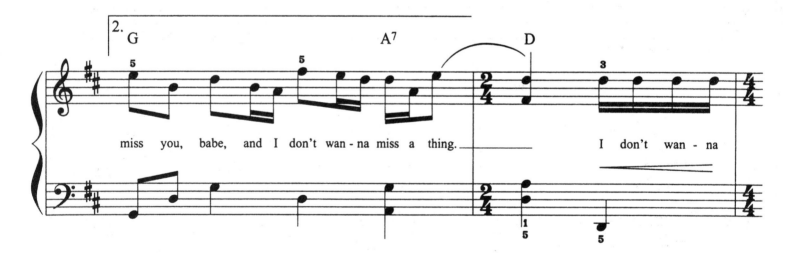

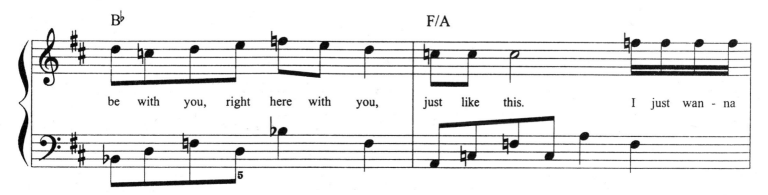

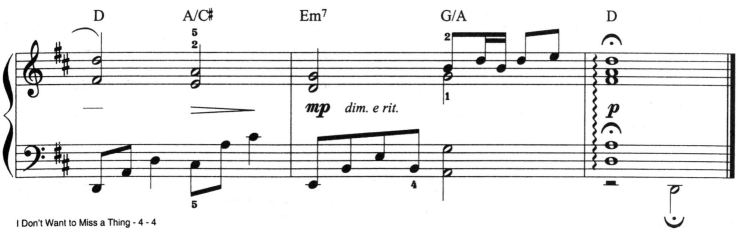

I Don't Want to Miss a Thing - 4 - 4

I STILL BELIEVE

Words and Music by
ANTONINA ARMATO and
BEPPE CANTORELLI
Arranged by DAN COATES

I Still Believe - 4 - 1

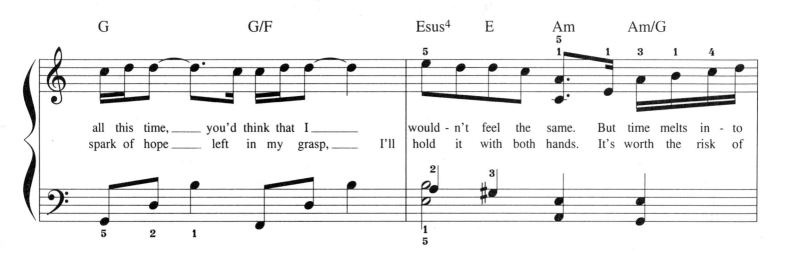

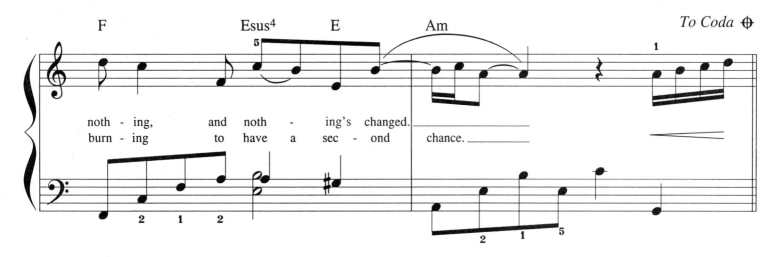

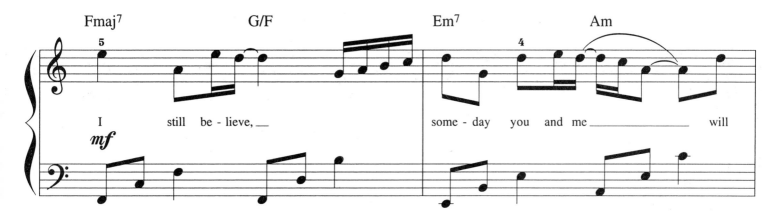

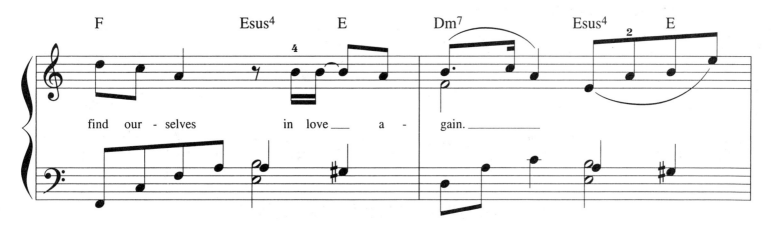

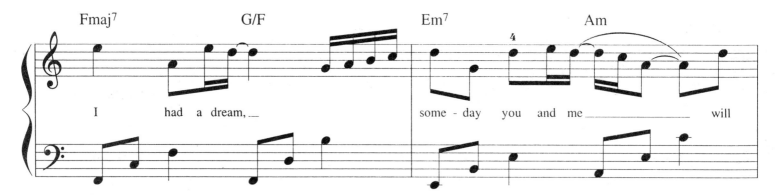

I had a dream, ___ some-day you and me _____ will

find our-selves in love __ a - gain. _____ Each day of my

D.S. 𝄋 *al Coda*

Coda

No, no, __ no, __ no, I need you, ba - by.

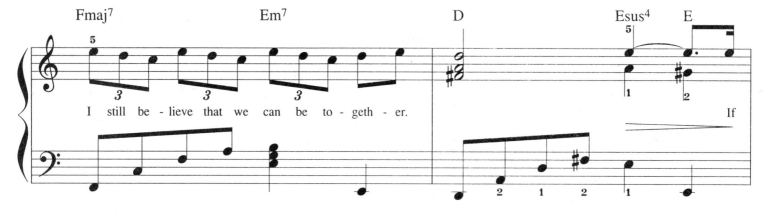

I still be - lieve that we can be to - geth - er. If

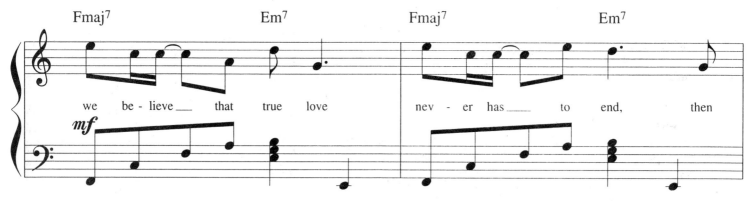

we be - lieve __ that true love nev - er has __ to end, then

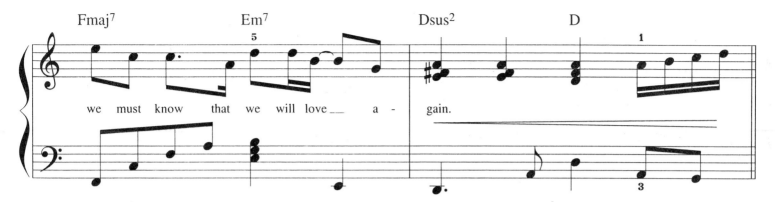

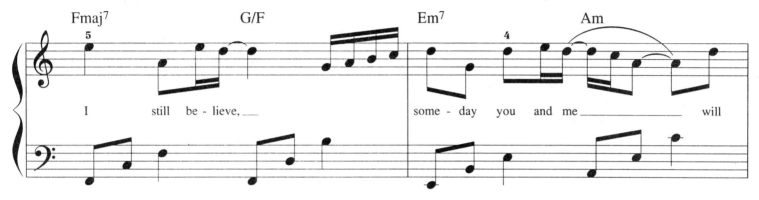

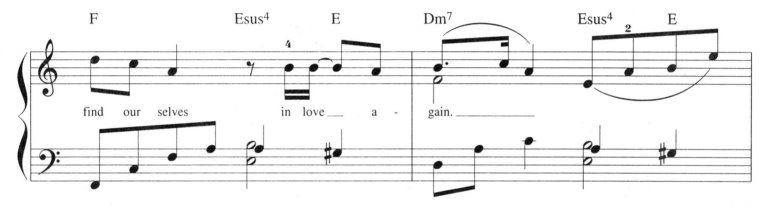

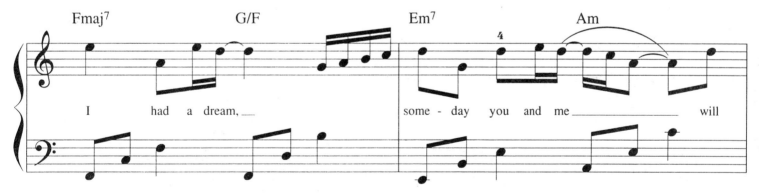

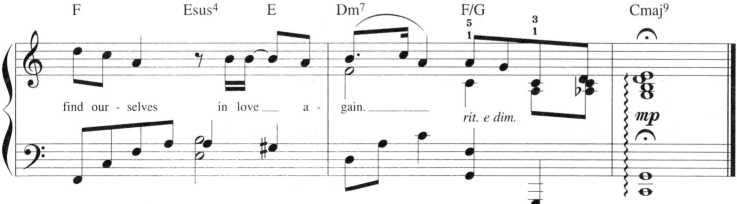

I Still Believe - 4 - 4

I WANT IT THAT WAY

Words and Music by
MAX MARTIN and ANDREAS CARLSSON
Arranged by DAN COATES

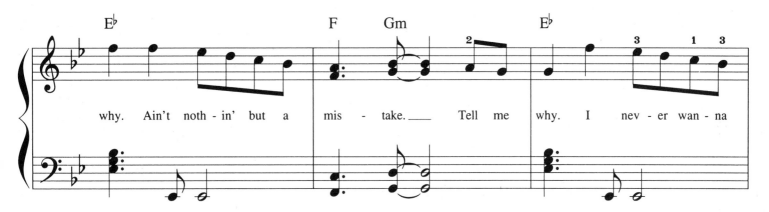

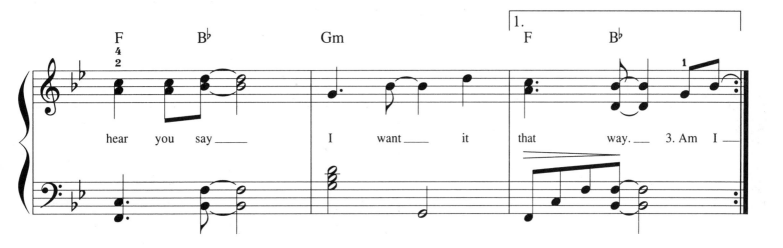

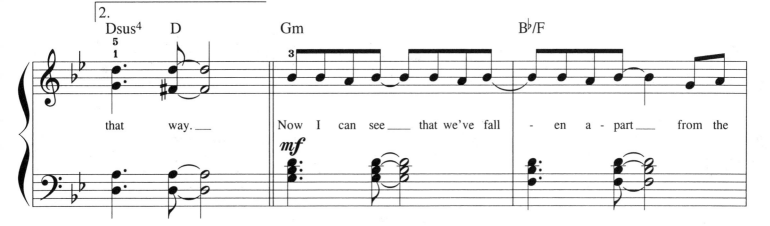

I Want It That Way - 4 - 2

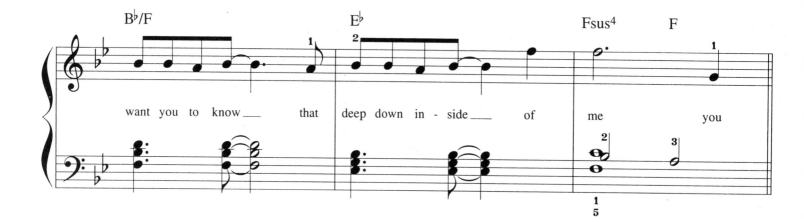

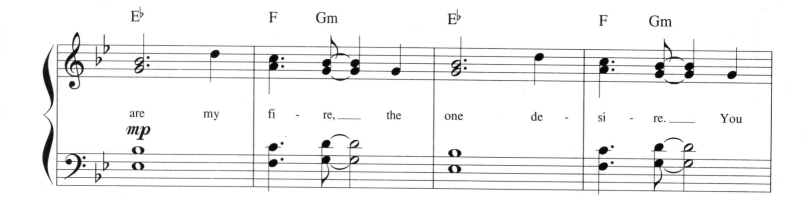

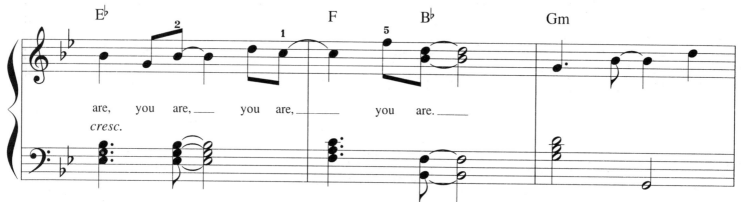

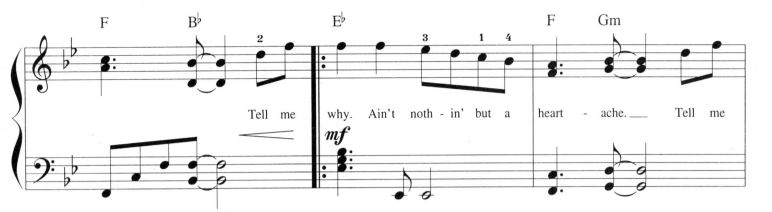

Verse 3:
Am I your fire,
Your one desire?
I know it's too late,
But I want it that way.
(To Chorus:)

I'LL NEVER BREAK YOUR HEART

By
ALBERT MANNO and
EUGENE WILDE
Arranged by DAN COATES

Moderately slow ♩. = 66

1. From the first day that I saw your smil-ing face, hon-ey, I

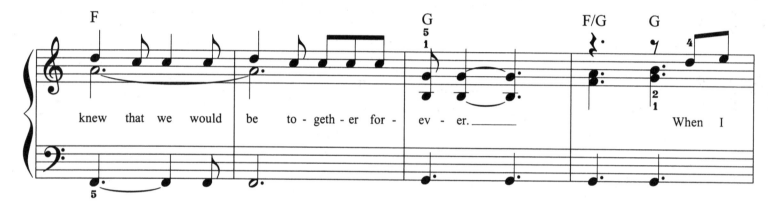

knew that we would be to-geth-er for-ev-er._____ When I

ask_____ you_____ out, you said no, but I found out,_____ dar-ling,

that you'd been hurt, you felt that you'd nev-er love a-gain._____

I'll Never Break Your Heart - 4 - 1

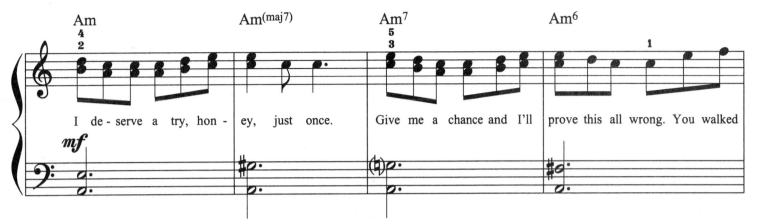

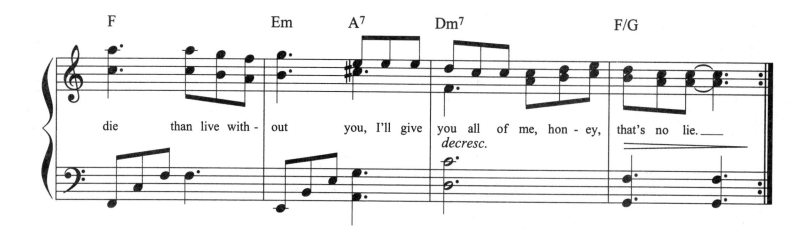

break your _____ heart, I'll nev - er make you _____ cry. I'd rath - er

die than live with - out you, I'll give you all of me, hon - ey, that's no lie. ____

decresc.

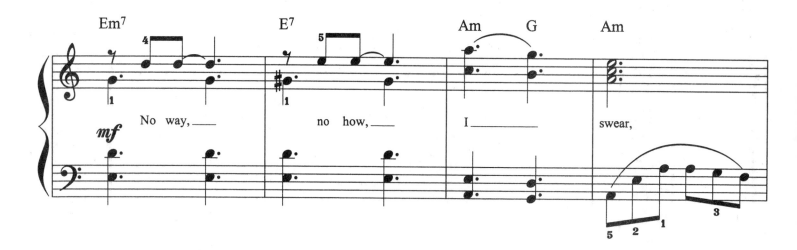

mf No way, ____ no how, ____ I _____ swear,

no way, ____ no how. ____ I, I'll nev - er

cresc.

Verse 2:
As I walked by you,
Will you get to know me
A little more better?
Girl, that's the way love goes.
And I know you're afraid
To let your feelings show,
And I understand.
But girl, it's time to let go.
I deserve a try, honey,
Just once,
Give me a chance
And I'll prove this all wrong.
You walked in,
You were so quick to judge.
But, honey, he's nothing like me.
(To Chorus:)

I'LL STILL LOVE YOU MORE

Words and Music by
DIANE WARREN

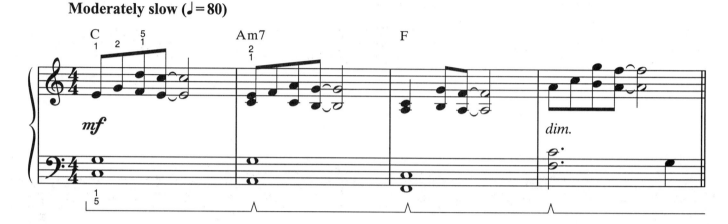

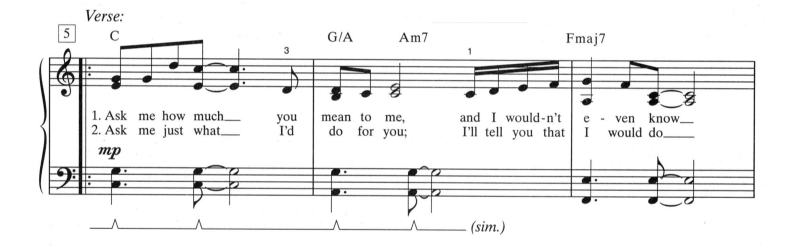

I'll Still Love You More - 5 - 1

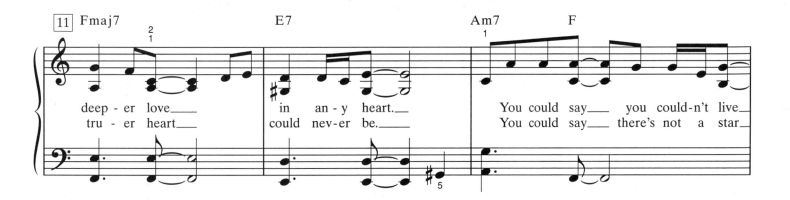

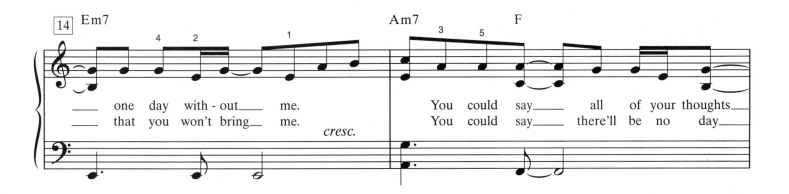

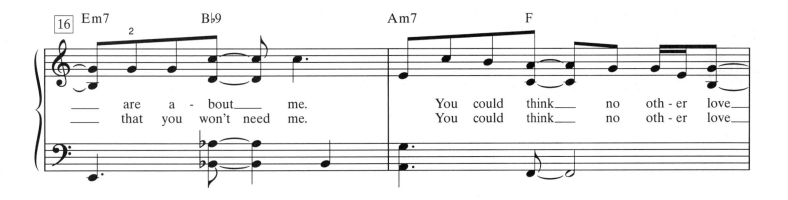

Chorus:

say that you love__ me more than an-y-bod__-y than an-y-one's ev__-__ er been loved__

____ be-fore, as much as you love__ me, ba-by, I'll still love you, ba-by,

I'll still love you more.__

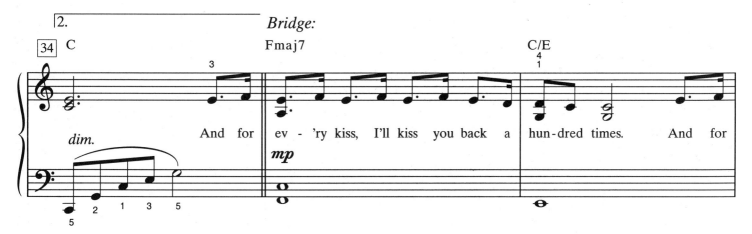

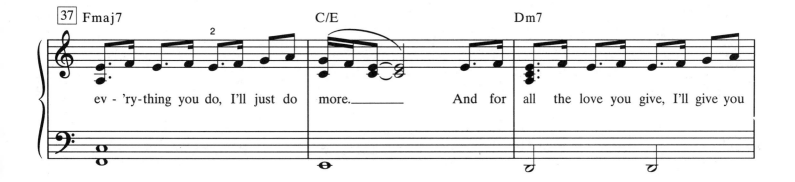

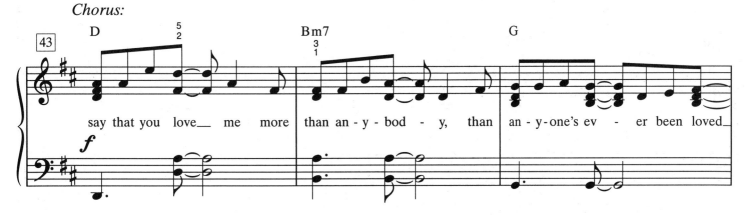

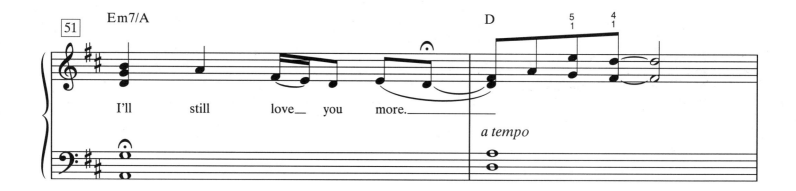

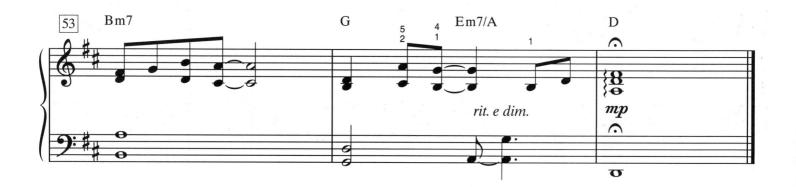

LOST IN YOU

Words and Music by
TOMMY SIMS, GORDON KENNEDY
and WAYNE KIRKPATRICK

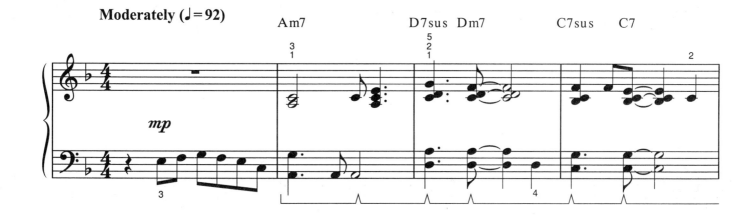

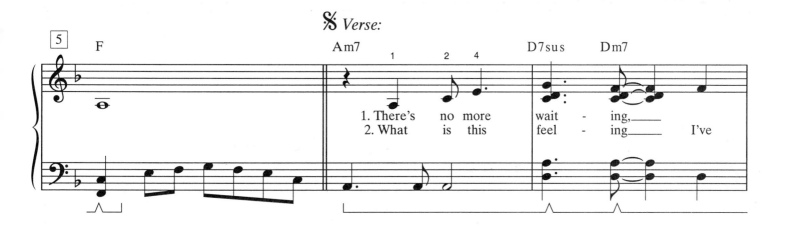

Chorus:

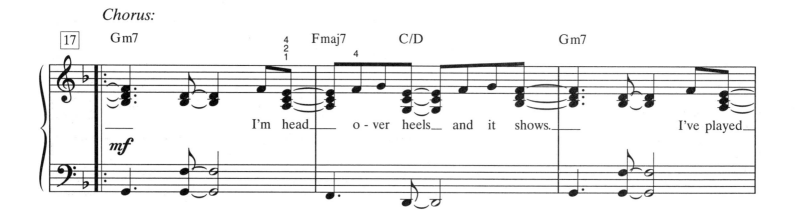

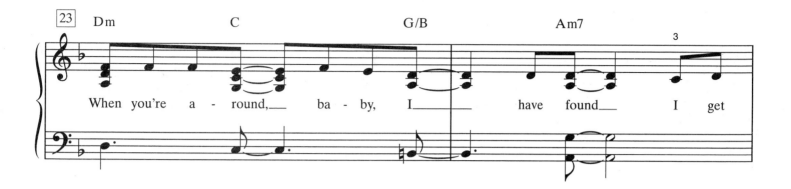

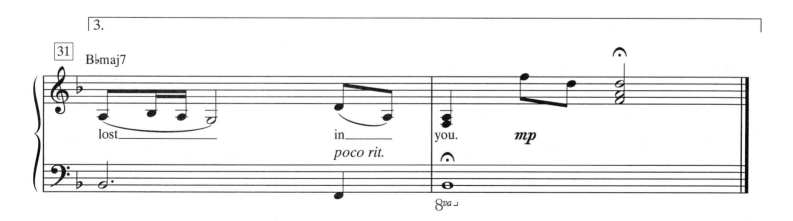

LARGER THAN LIFE

Words and Music by
MAX MARTIN, KRISTIAN LUNDIN
and BRIAN T. LITTRELL
Arranged by DAN COATES

Steady rock beat ♩ = 120

Verse:

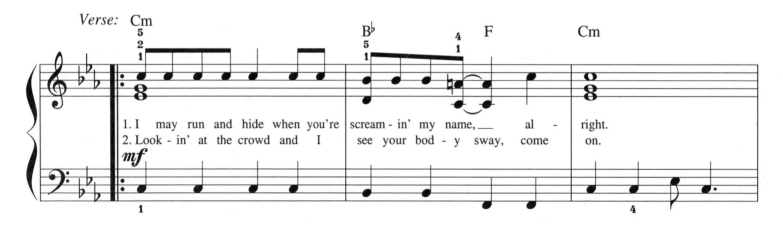

1. I may run and hide when you're scream-in' my name, __ al - right.
2. Look-in' at the crowd and I see your bod - y sway, come on.

But let me tell you now there are pric - es to fame, __ al -
Wish - in' I could thank you in a dif - fer - ent way, __ come

Larger Than Life - 4 - 1

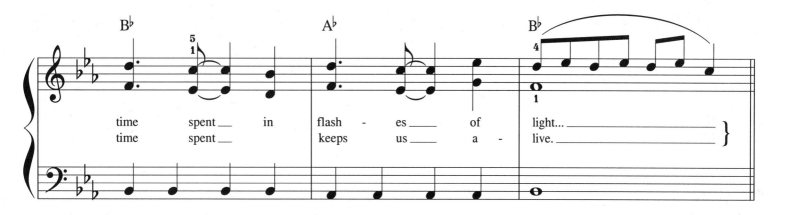

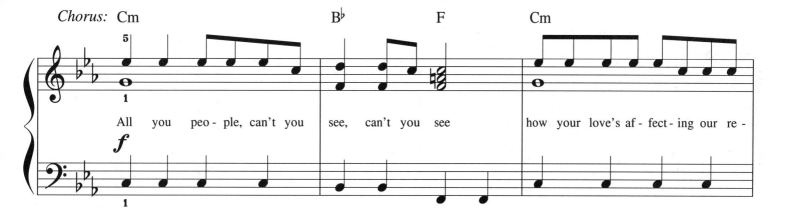

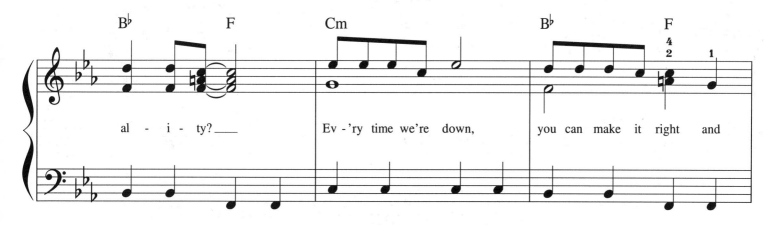

108

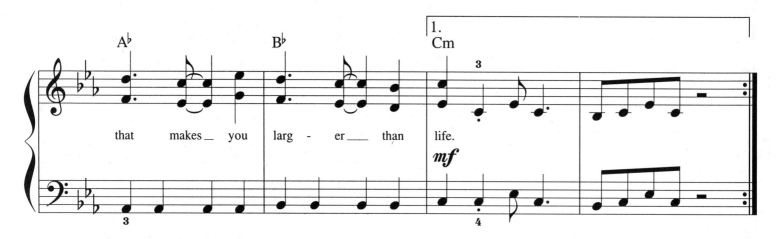

that makes__ you larg - er ____ than life.

life.

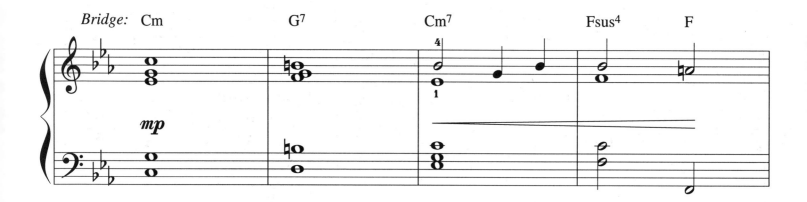

Bridge: Cm   G⁷   Cm⁷   Fsus⁴   F

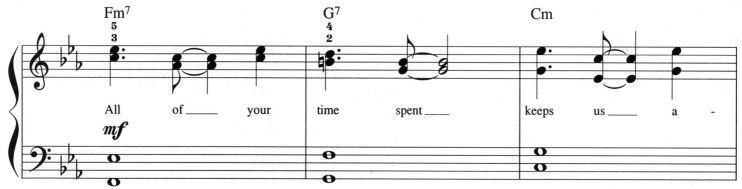

Fm⁷   G⁷   Cm

All   of ____ your   time   spent ____   keeps   us ____ a -

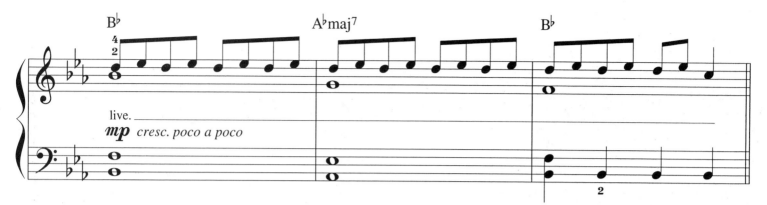

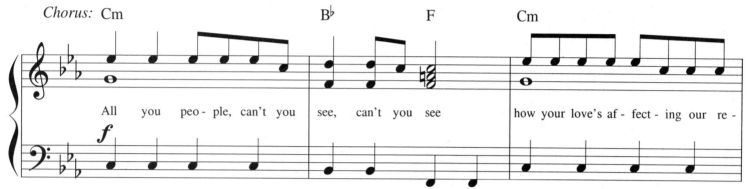

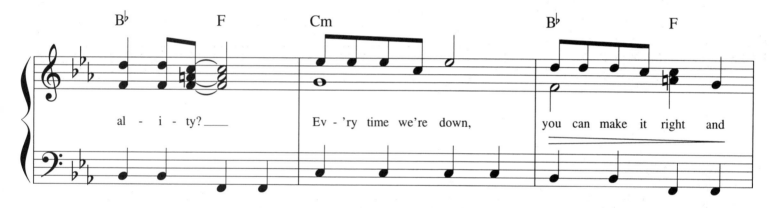

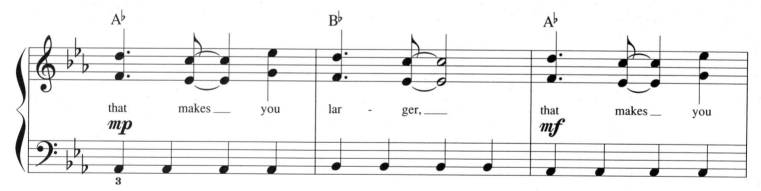

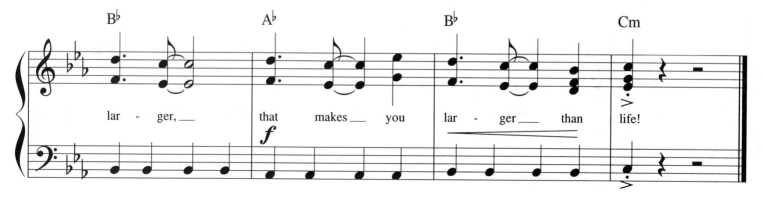

Larger Than Life - 4 - 4

LET ME LET GO

Arranged by
JOHN BRIMHALL

Words and Music by
DENNIS MORGAN and
STEVE DIAMOND

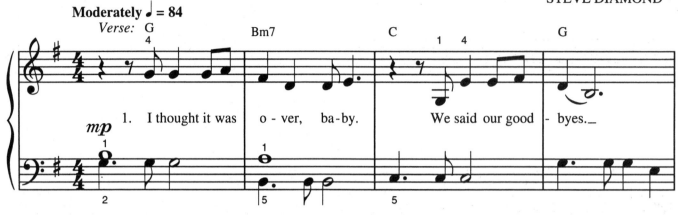

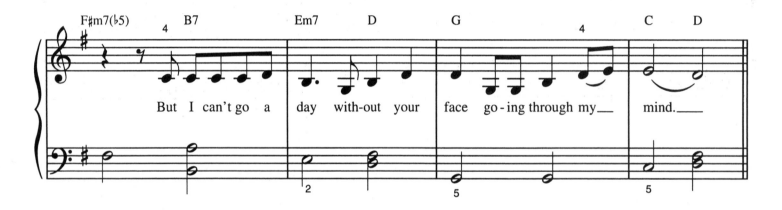

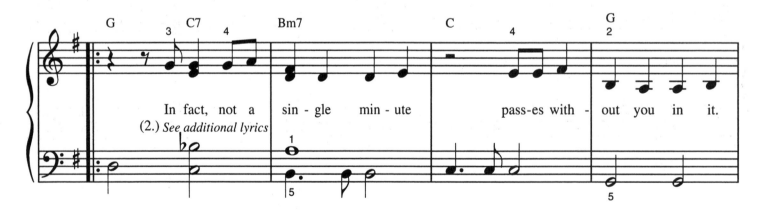

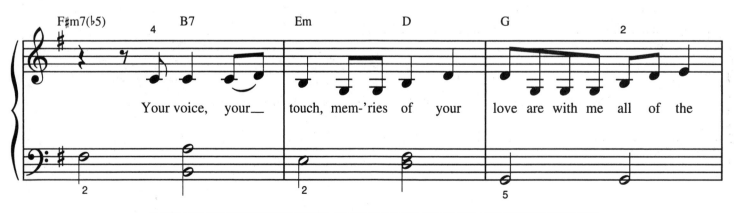

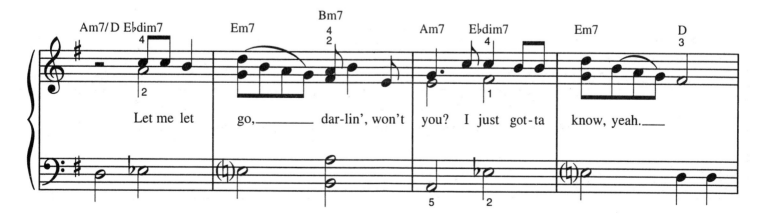

112

If this is for the best, why are you still in my heart, are you still in my

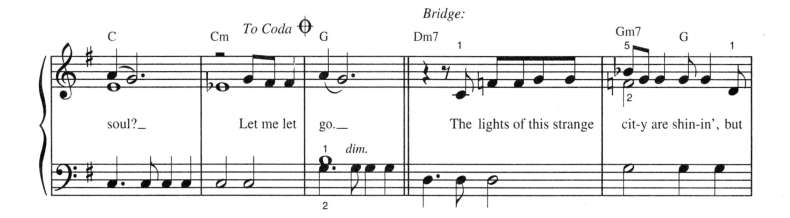

soul?_ Let me let go._ *Bridge:* The lights of this strange cit-y are shin-in', but

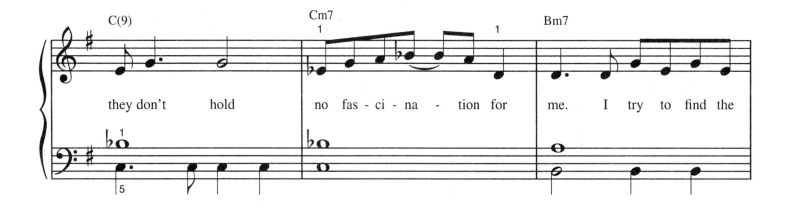

they don't hold no fas-ci-na - tion for me. I try to find the

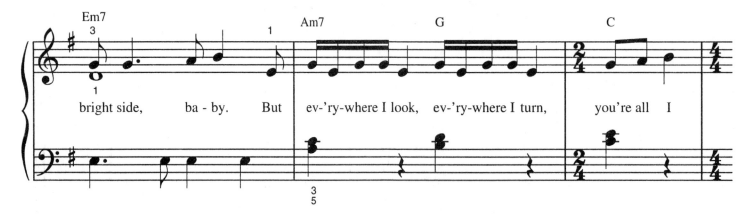

bright side, ba - by. But ev-'ry-where I look, ev-'ry-where I turn, you're all I

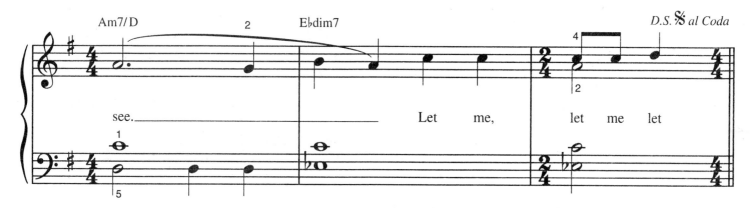

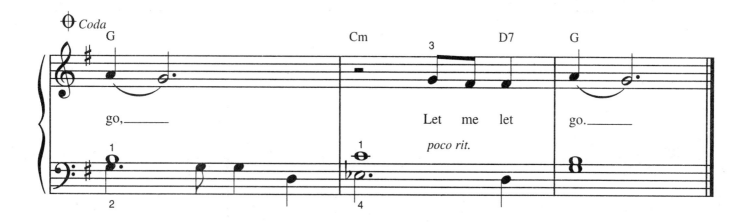

Verse 2:
I talked to you the other day.
Looks like you made your escape.
You put us behind;
No matter how I try, I can't do the same.
Let me let go, baby, let me let go. It just isn't right;
I've been two thousand miles down a dead end road.
(To Chorus:)

(God Must Have Spent)
A LITTLE MORE TIME ON YOU

Words and Music by
CARL STURKEN and EVAN ROGERS
Arranged by DAN COATES

Gently, with expression

(God Must Have Spent) a Little More Time on You - 4 - 1

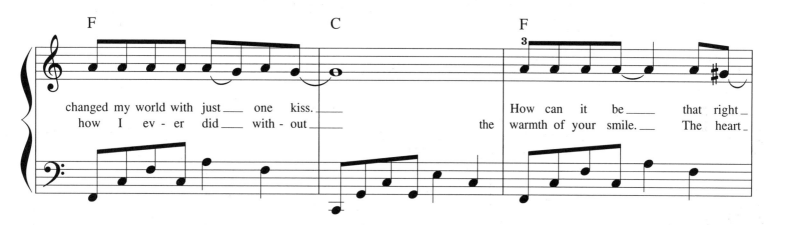

(God Must Have Spent) a Little More Time on You - 4 - 2

116

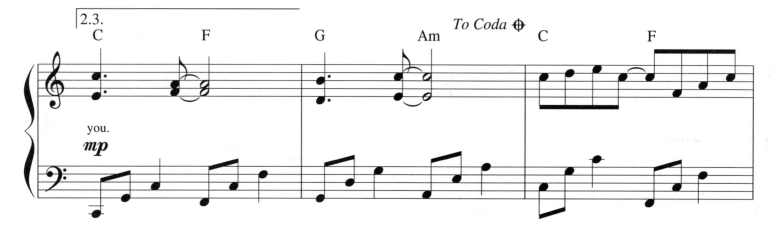

(God Must Have Spent) a Little More Time on You - 4 - 3

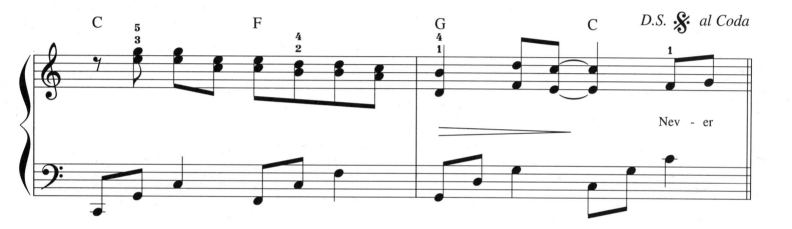

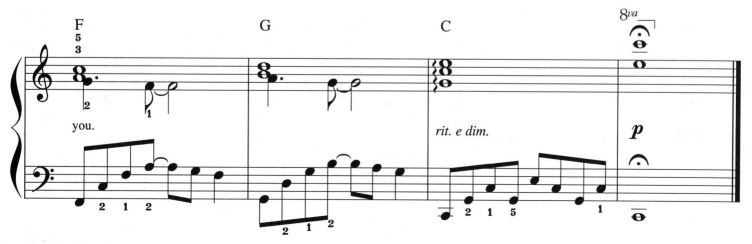

(God Must Have Spent) a Little More Time on You - 4 - 4

LIVIN' LA VIDA LOCA

Words and Music by
ROBI ROSA and DESMOND CHILD
Arranged by DAN COATES

Fast ♩ = 174

1. She's in - to su - per - sti - tions, black cats and voo - doo dolls. ___

I feel a pre - mo - ni - tion, that girl's gon - na make me fall. ___

Livin' La Vida Loca - 6 - 1

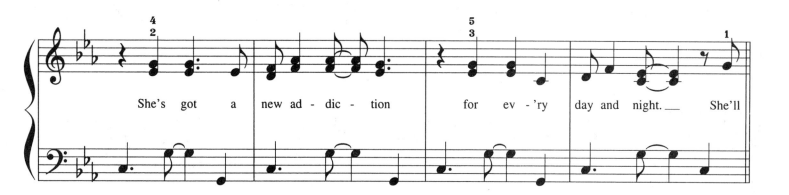

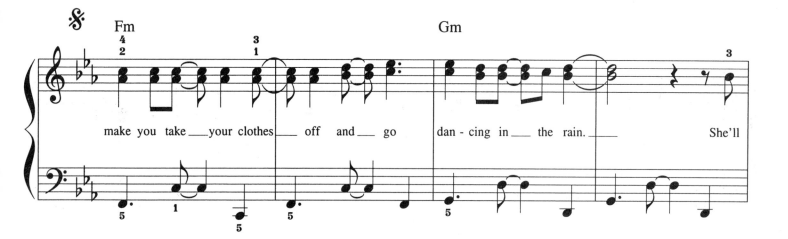

120

like a bul-let to _____ your brain.

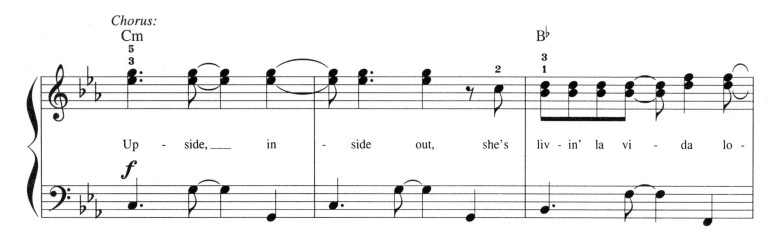

Chorus:

Up-side, _____ in - side out, she's liv-in' la vi - da lo-

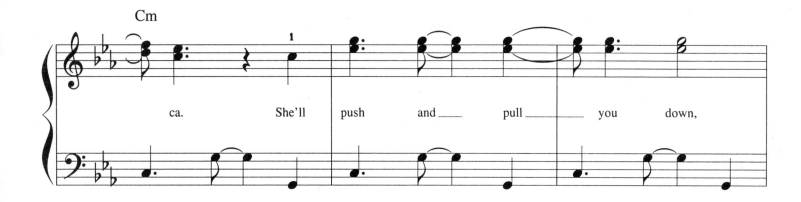

ca. She'll push and _____ pull _____ you down,

liv - in' la vi - da lo - ca. Her lips are _____ dev-

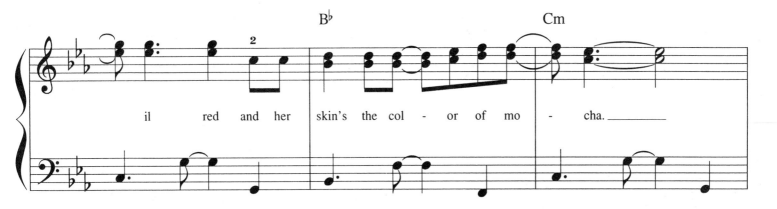

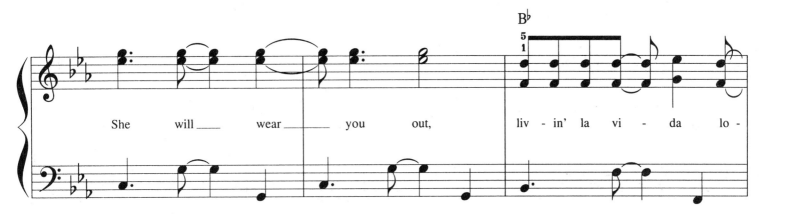

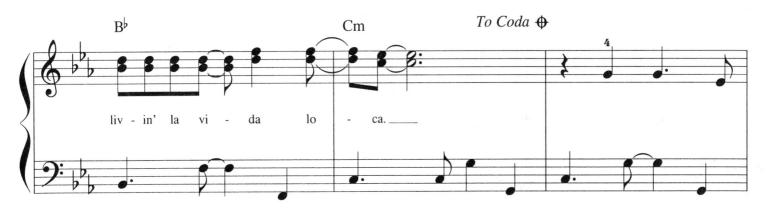

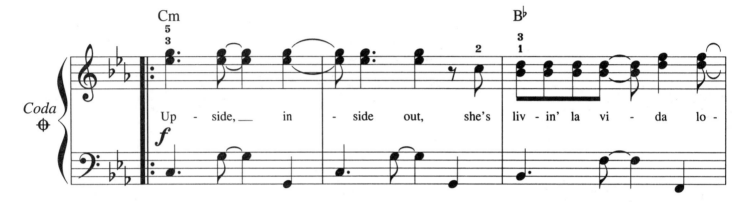

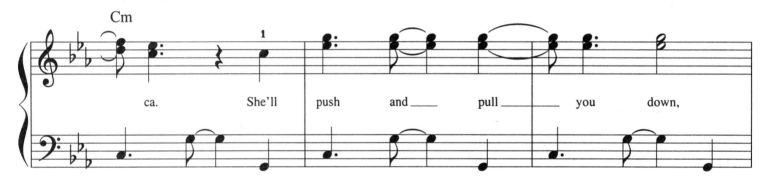

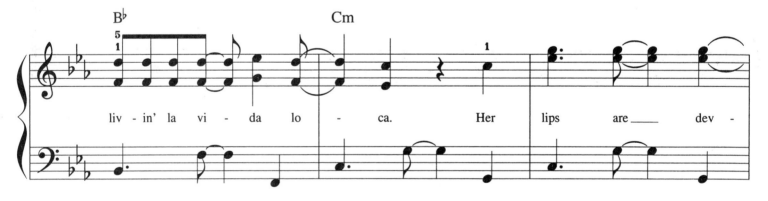

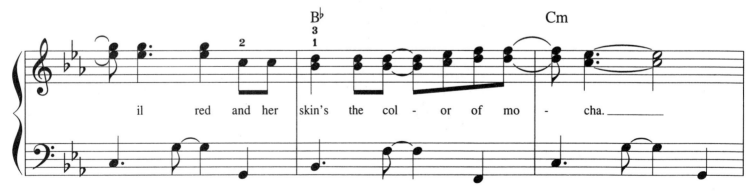

Livin' La Vida Loca - 6 - 5

She will ___ wear ___ you out, liv - in' la vi - da lo -

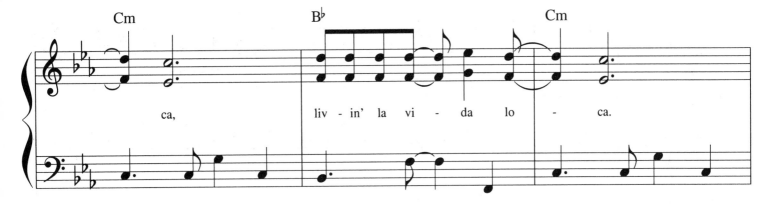

ca, liv - in' la vi - da lo - ca.

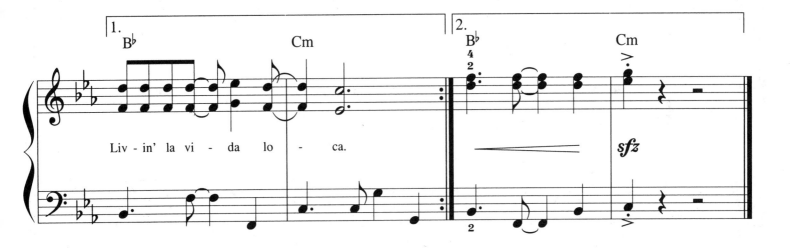

1.

Liv - in' la vi - da lo - ca.

2.

Verse 3:
Woke up in New York City
In a funky, cheap hotel.
She took my heart and she took my money.
She must have slipped me a sleeping pill.

She never drinks the water
And makes you order French champagne.
Once you've had a taste of her
You'll never be the same.
Yeah, she'll make you go insane.
(To Chorus:)

LOVE LIKE OURS

Lyrics by
ALAN and MARILYN BERGMAN

Music by
DAVE GRUSIN
Arranged by DAN COATES

Slowly, with feeling

mp legato

I look at you and

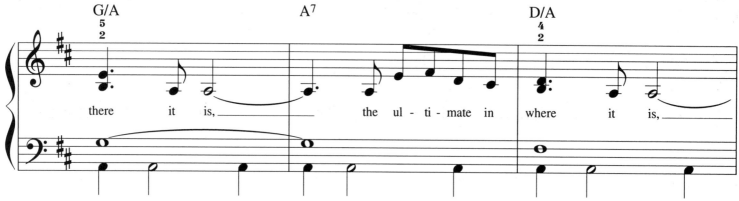

there it is, the ul - ti - mate in where it is,

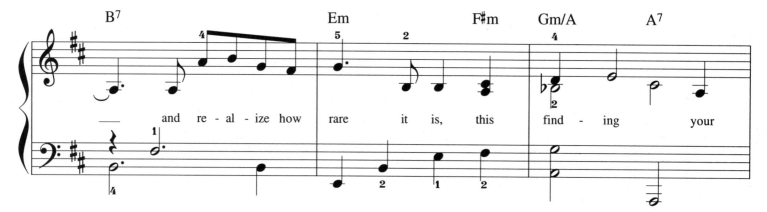

and re - al - ize how rare it is, this find - ing your

love. You try so man - y arms when you are

Love Like Ours - 3 - 1

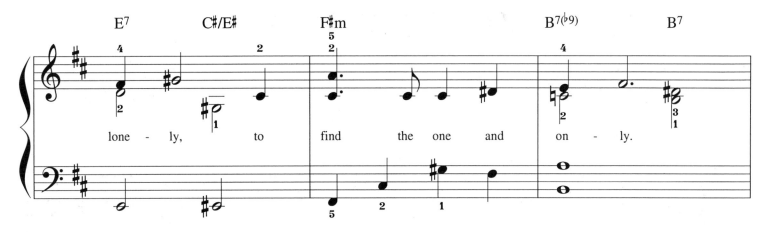

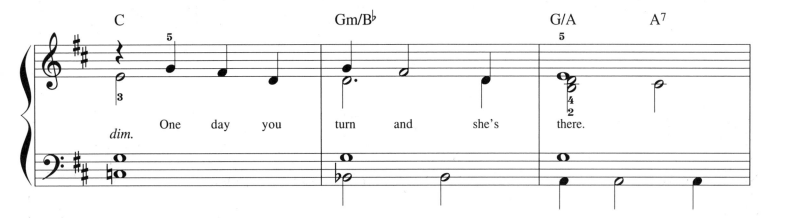

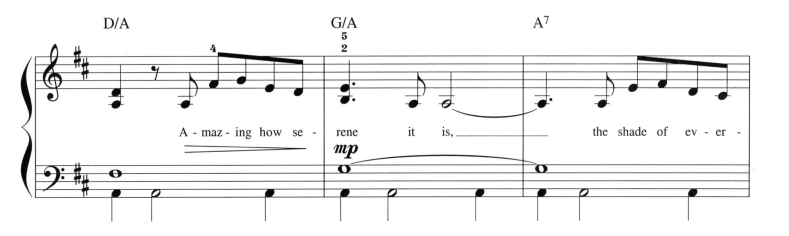

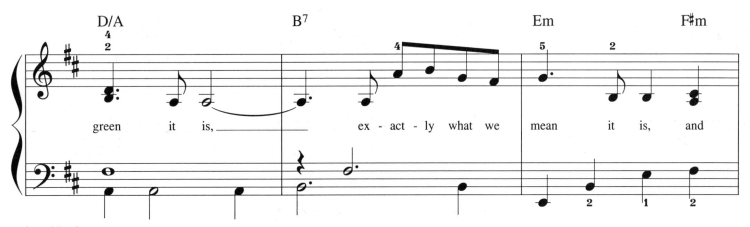

THE PRAYER

Words and Music by
CAROLE BAYER SAGER and DAVID FOSTER
Italian Lyric by ALBERTO TESTA and TONY RENIS
Arranged by DAN COATES

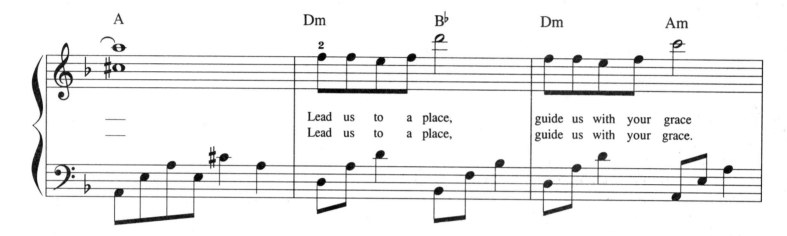

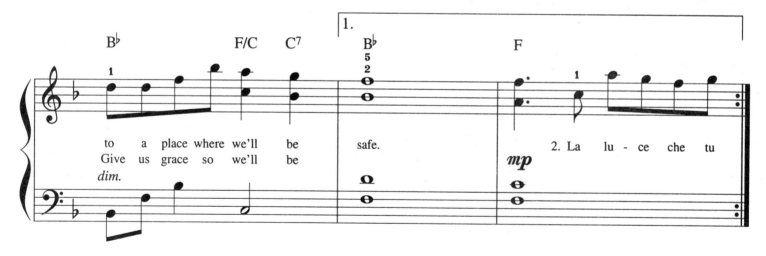

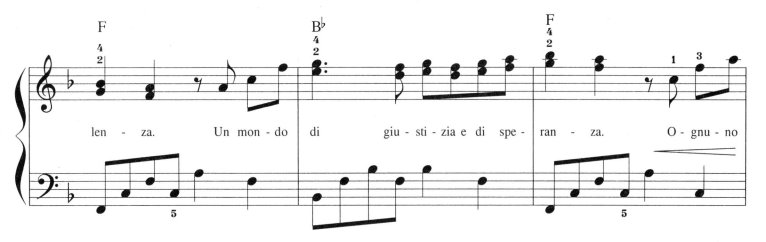

len - za. Un mon - do di giu - sti - zia e di spe - ran - za. O - gnu - no

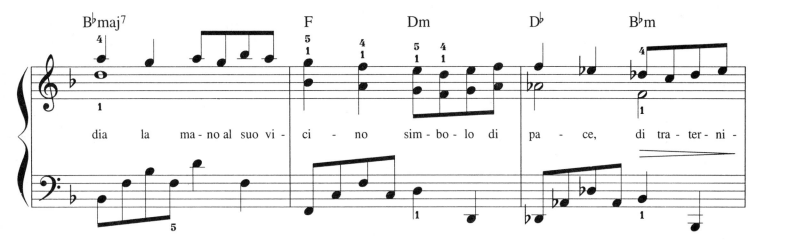

dia la ma - no al suo vi - ci - no sim - bo - lo di pa - ce, di tra - ter - ni -

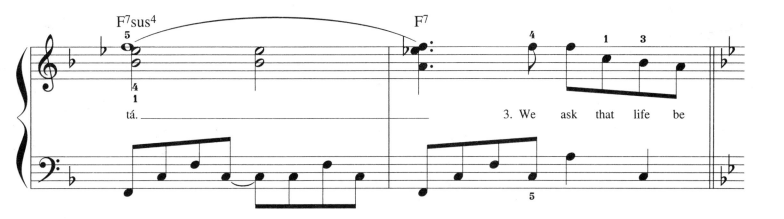

tá. _____ 3. We ask that life be

kind,

mp

and watch us from a - bove.

130

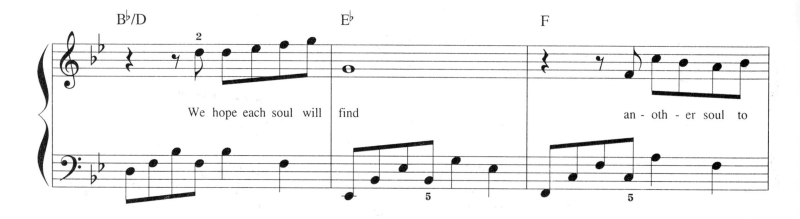

We hope each soul will find an - oth - er soul to

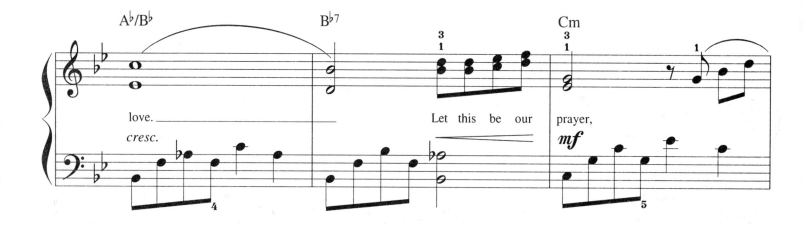

love. _____ Let this be our prayer,

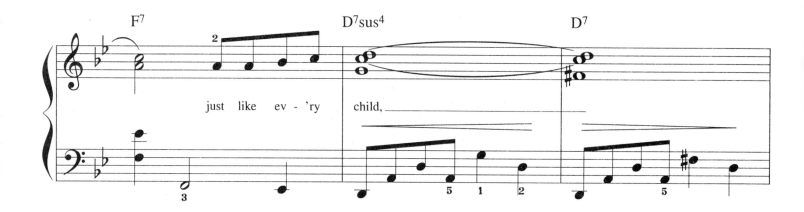

just like ev - 'ry child, _____

need to find a place, guide us with your grace. Give us faith so we'll be

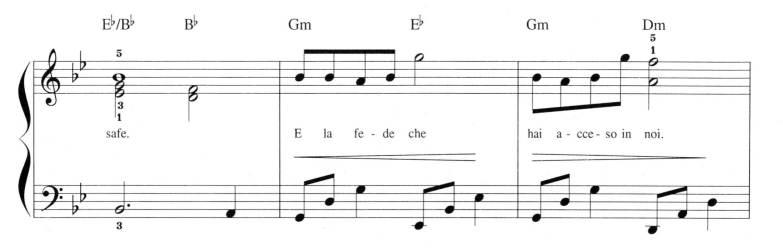

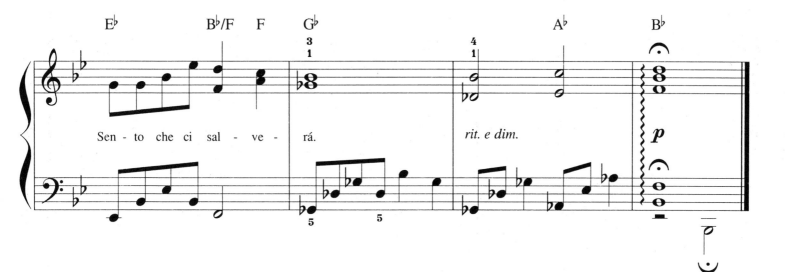

Verse 2 (English lyric):
I pray we'll find your light,
And hold it in our hearts
When stars go out each night.
Let this be our prayer,
When shadows fill our day.
Lead us to a place,
Guide us with your grace.
Give us faith so we'll be safe.

Verse 3 (Italian lyric):
La forza che ci dai
é il desiderio che.
Ognuno trovi amore
Intorno e dentro sé.
(Chorus:)

MAN! I FEEL LIKE A WOMAN!

Arranged by
JOHN BRIMHALL

Words and Music by
SHANIA TWAIN and R.J. LANGE

Man! I Feel Like a Woman! - 4 - 1

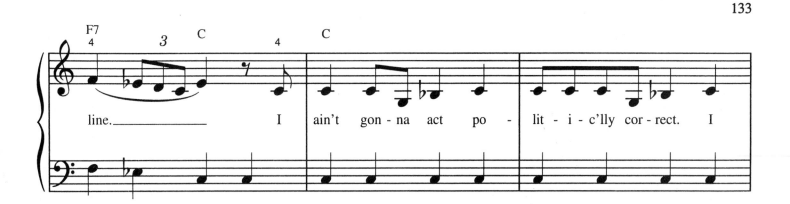

line._____ I ain't gon - na act po - lit - i - c'lly cor - rect. I

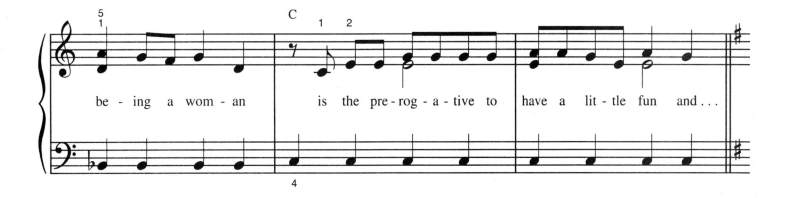

on - ly wan - na have a good time._____ The best thing a - bout__

be - ing a wom - an is the pre - rog - a - tive to have a lit - tle fun and . . .

Chorus:

Oh, oh, oh, go to - tal - ly cra - zy,___ for - get I'm a la - dy.___

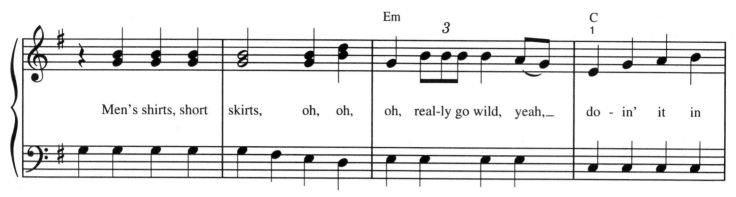

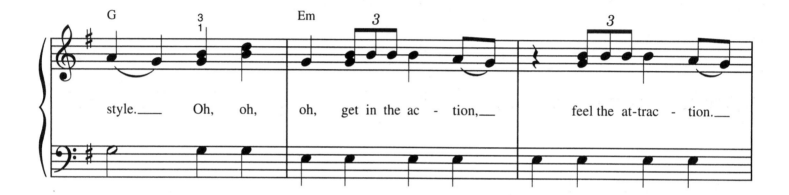

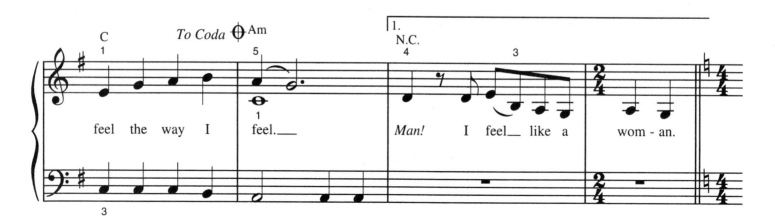

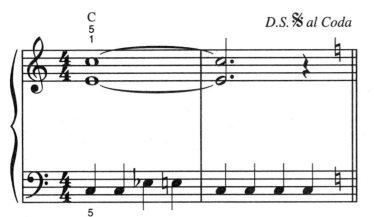

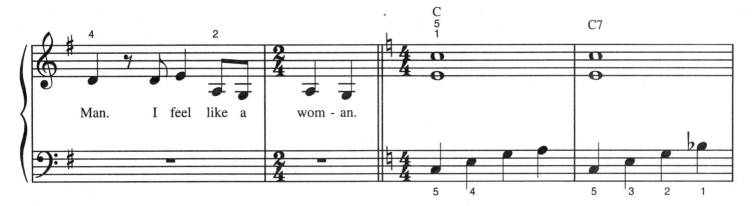

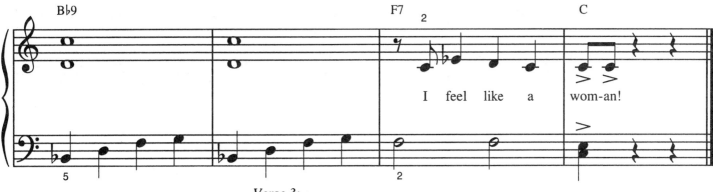

Verse 3:
The girls need a break.
Tonight we're gonna take
The chance to get out on the town.
We don't need romance.
We only wanna dance.
We're gonna let our hair hang down.
The best thing about being a woman
Is the prerogative to have a little fun and . . .
(To Chorus:)

From the Miramax Motion Picture "Music Of The Heart"

MUSIC OF MY HEART

Words and Music by
DIANE WARREN
Arranged by DAN COATES

Slowly, with feeling

1. You'll nev - er know _____ what you've
2. You were the one _____ al - ways

done for me, _____ what your faith in me has
on my side, _____ al - ways stand - ing by,

done for my soul. _____ You'll nev - er know ___ the gift you've
see - ing me through. _____ You were the song ___ that al - ways

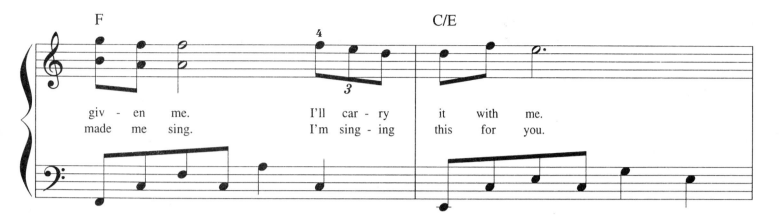

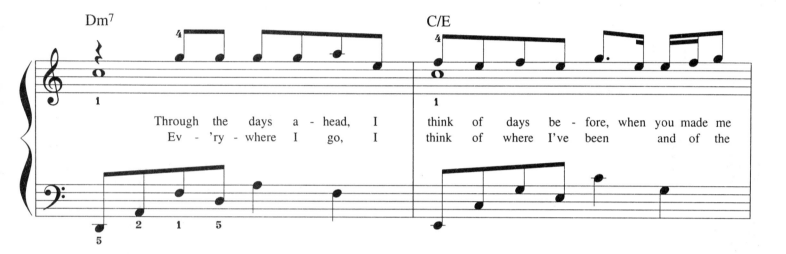

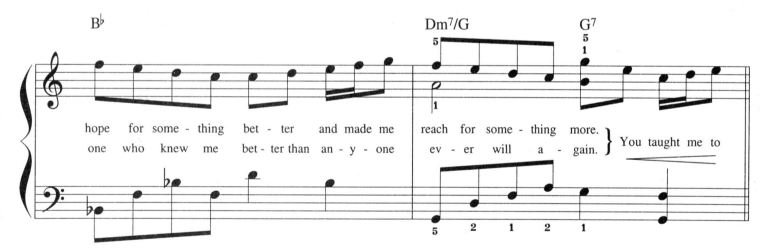

Music of My Heart - 4 - 2

137

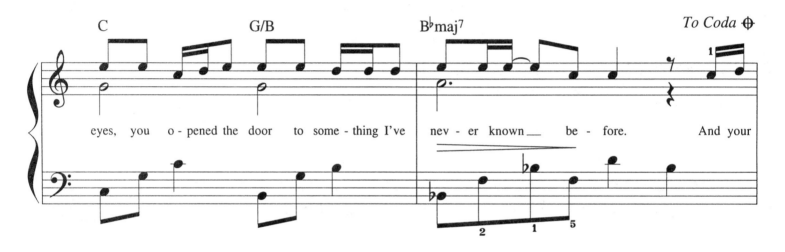

NO SCRUBS

Words and Music by
KEVIN BRIGGS, KANDI BURRIS
and TAMEKA COTTLE

%S   *Chorus:*

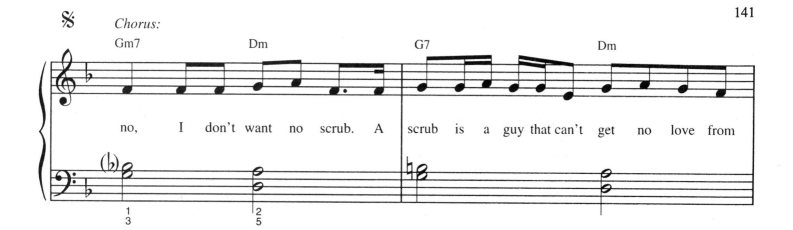

no,   I   don't want   no   scrub.   A   scrub   is   a   guy that can't   get   no   love from

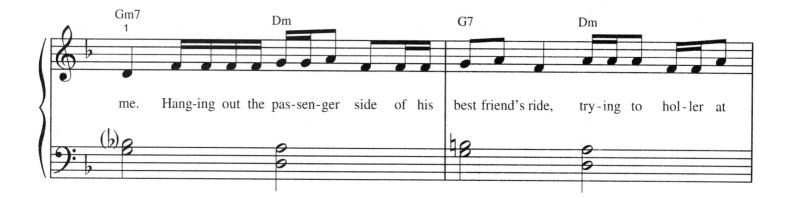

me.   Hang-ing out the pas-sen-ger   side   of his   best friend's ride,   try-ing to hol-ler at

me.   I   don't want   no   scrub.   A   scrub   is   a   guy that can't   get   no   love from

me.   Hang-in' out the pas-sen-ger   side   of his   best friend's ride,   try-ing to hol-ler at

2. But a

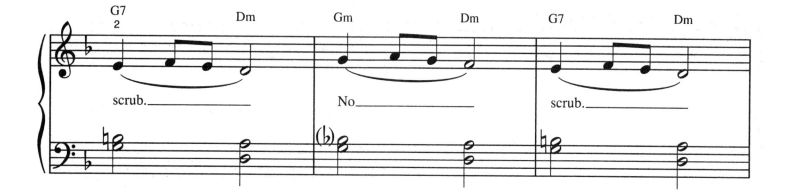

Verse 2:
But a scrub is checkin' me.
But his game is kinda weak.
And I know that he can't approach me,
'Cause I'm lookin' like class and he's lookin' like trash.
Can't get wit' no deadbeat ass. So
No, I don't want your number.
No, I don't want to give you mine.
No, I don't want to meet you nowhere.
No, I don't want none of your time.
And . . .
(To Chorus:)

NOTHING REALLY MATTERS

Words and Music by
MADONNA CICCONE and
PATRICK LEONARD
Arranged by DAN COATES

Moderate, steady beat ♩ = 104

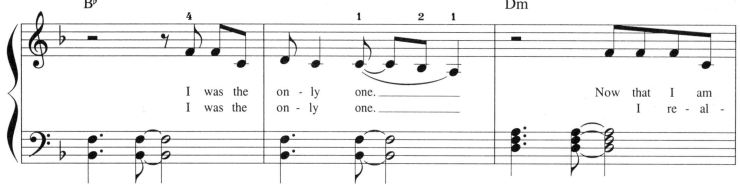

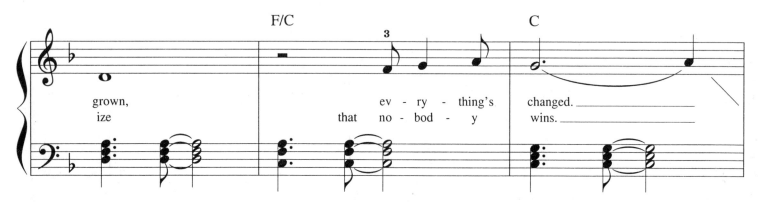

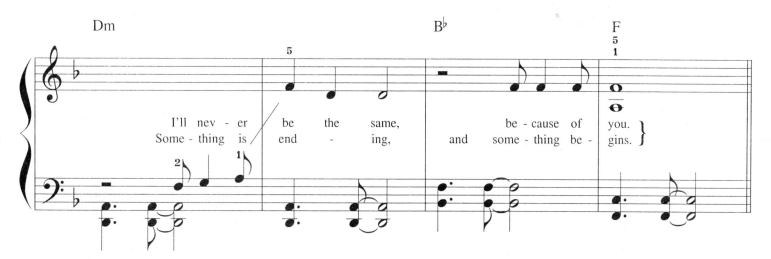

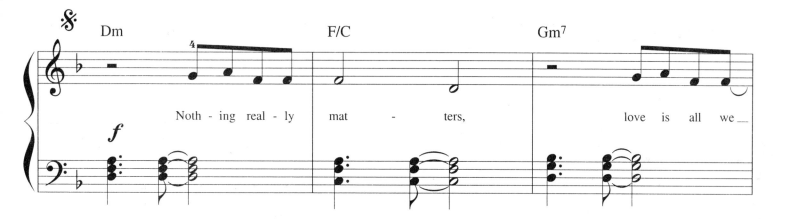

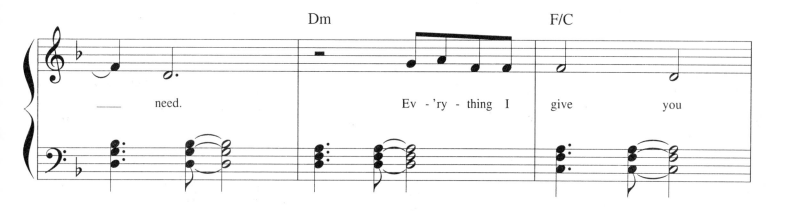

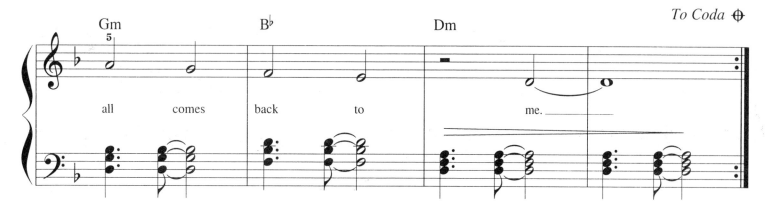

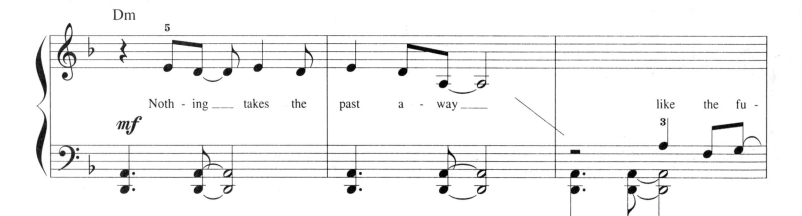

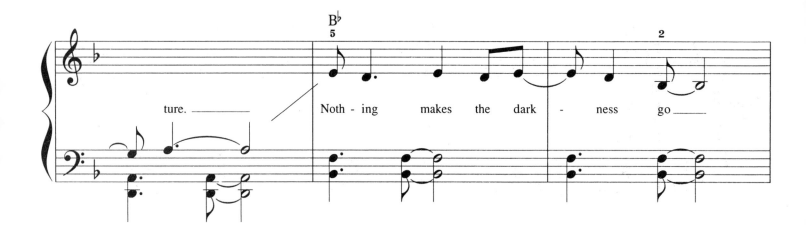

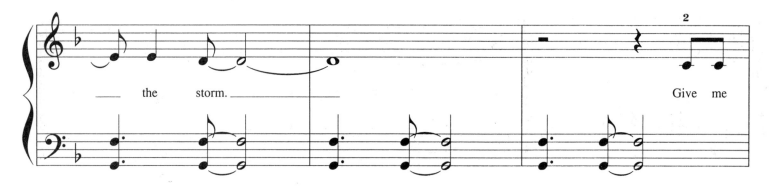

D.S. 𝄋 al Coda

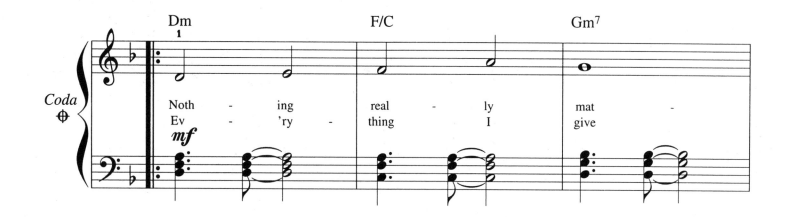

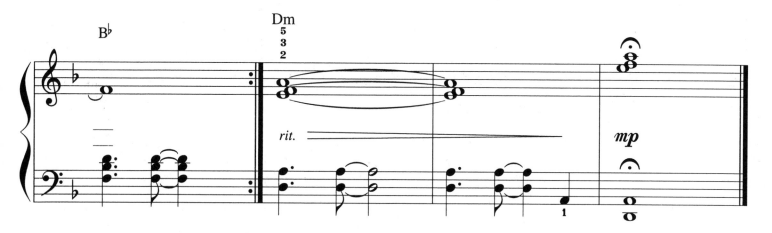

SHE'S ALL I EVER HAD

Words and Music by
ROBI ROSA, GEORGE NORIEGA
and JON SECADA
Arranged by DAN COATES

Moderately slow

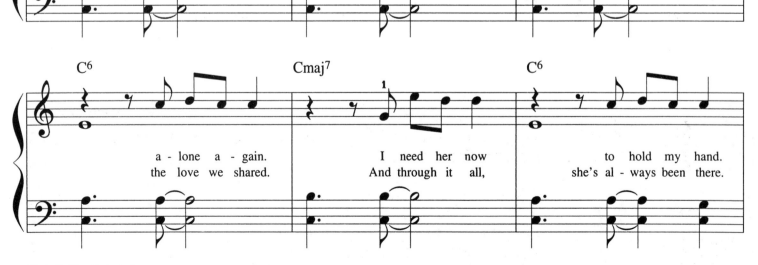

Lyrics:

1. Here I am, bro - ken wings.
2. So much time, so much pain, but

Qui - et thoughts, un - spo - ken dreams. Here I am,
there's one thing that still re - mains. It's the way she cared,

a - lone a - gain. I need her now to hold my hand.
the love we shared. And through it all, she's al - ways been there.

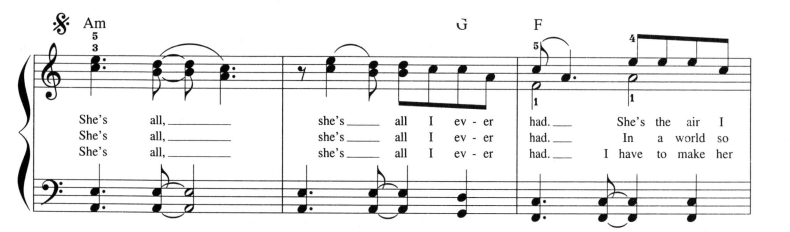

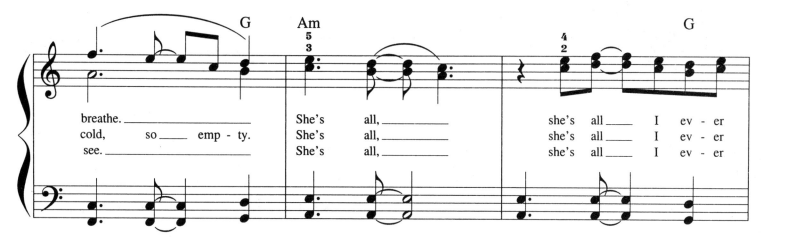

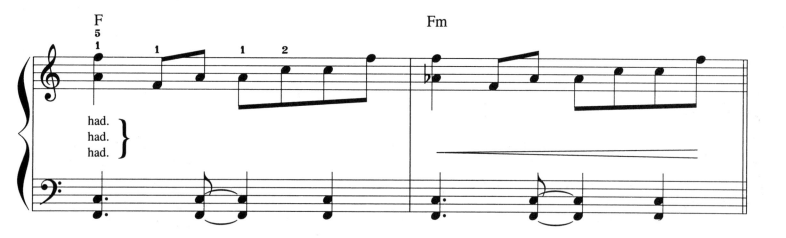

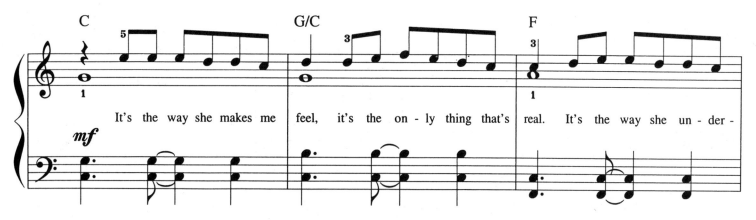

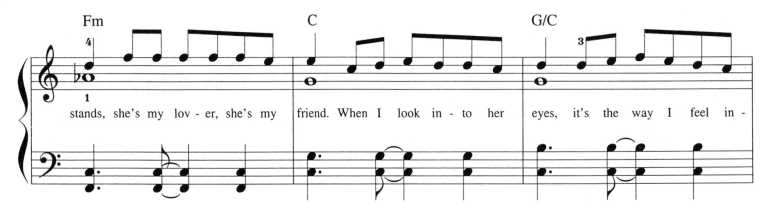

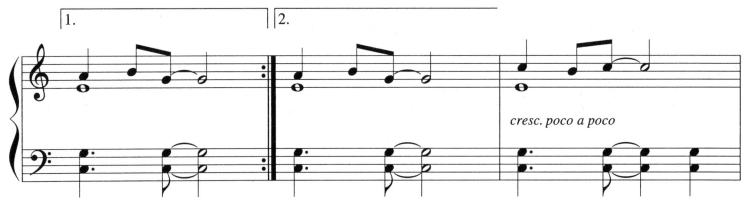

She's All I Ever Had - 4 - 3

She's All I Ever Had - 4 - 4

SOMETIMES

Words and Music by
JORGEN ELOFSSON
Arranged by DAN COATES

Sometimes - 4 - 1

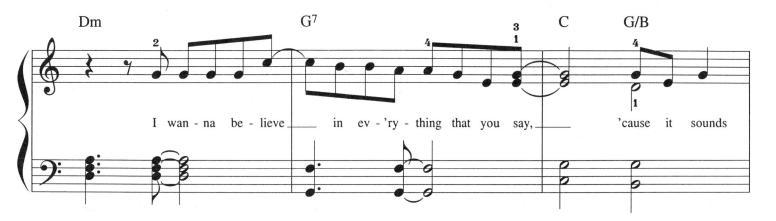

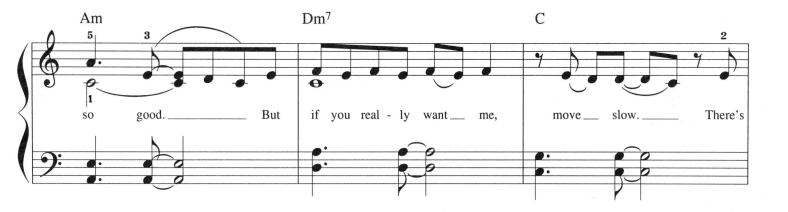

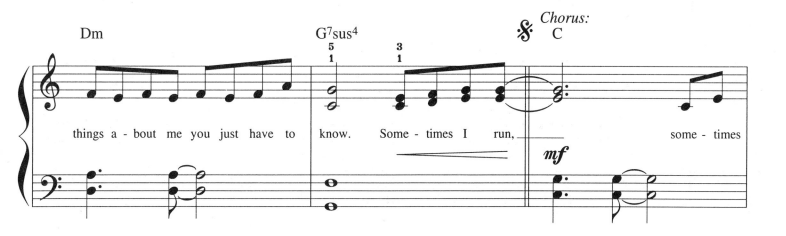

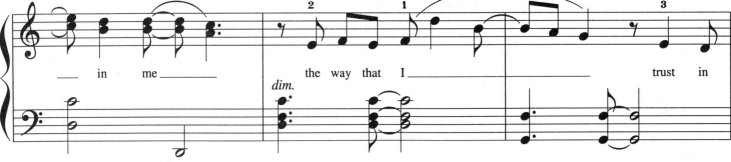

To Coda ⊕

C   G/B   Dm⁷

_____ you tight, _____ treat you right, be with you day _____ and night. _____

1.
G⁷

Ba - by, all I need is time.

2.
G⁷   C

All I real - ly want is to hold _____ you tight, _____ treat

G/B   Dm⁷   G⁷

you right, be with you day _____ and night. _____ Ba - by, all I need is time.

Bridge: F   E   Am

Just hang a - round and you'll see _____ there's no - where I'd rath - er be. _____ If you love me, trust

_f_

Dm⁷   G⁷

_____ in me _____ the way that I _____ trust in

dim.

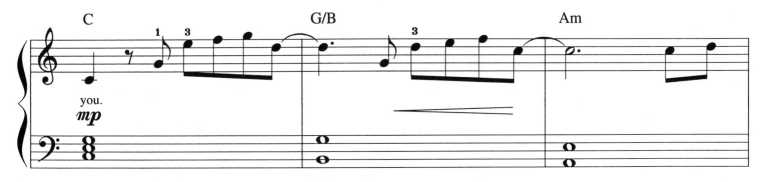

C   G/B   Am

you.

mp

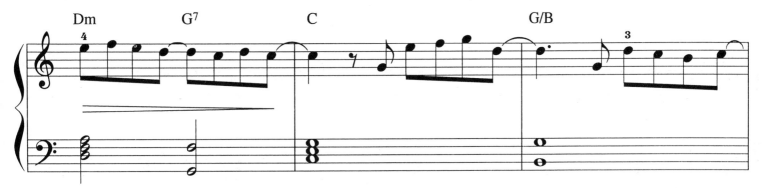

Dm   G⁷   C   G/B

D.S. 𝄋 al Coda

Am   Dm   G⁷

Some - times I run,

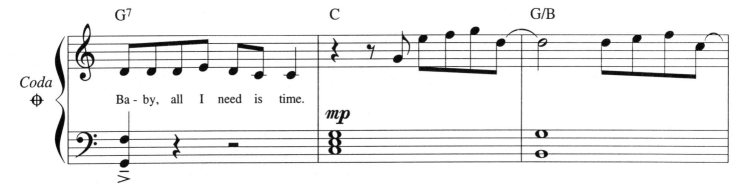

G⁷   C   G/B

Coda

Ba - by, all I need is time.

mp

Am   Dm   G⁷   C

rit. e dim.

p

SMOOTH

Lyrics by
ROB THOMAS

Music by ITAAL SHUR
and ROB THOMAS

Moderate latin rock (♩ = 112)

Verse:

hot one,
2. *See additional lyrics*

like sev-en in-ches from the mid-day sun.___

1. Man, it's a

Smooth - 5 - 1

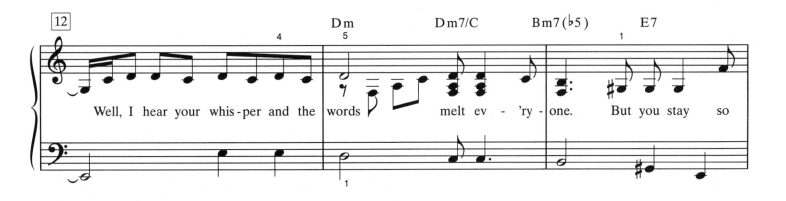

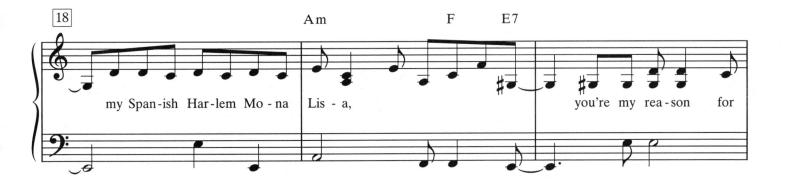

158

And if you said this life ain't good e-nough,___ I would give

my world to lift you up.___ I could change my life to

bet-ter suit___ your___ mood,___ 'cause you're so smooth.

Chorus:

Oh, and it's just like the o - cean

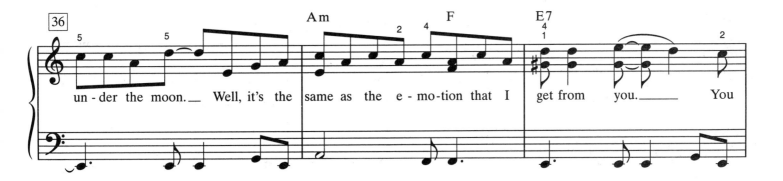

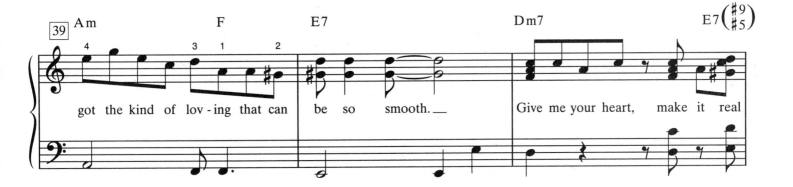

Verse 2:
Well, I'll tell you one thing,
If you would leave, it be a crying shame.
In every breath and every word
I hear your name calling me out, yeah.
Well, out from the barrio,
You hear my rhythm on your radio.
You feel the tugging of the world,
So soft and slow, turning you 'round and 'round.

And if you said
This life ain't good enough,
I would give my world to lift you up.
I could change my life
To better suit your mood,
'Cause you're so smooth.
(To Chorus:)

SPECIAL

Words and Music by
DOUG ERIKSON, SHIRLEY MANSON,
STEVE MARKER and BUTCH VIG

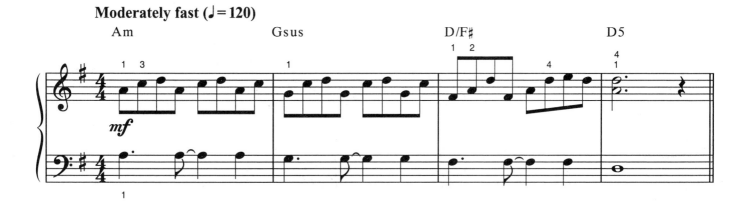

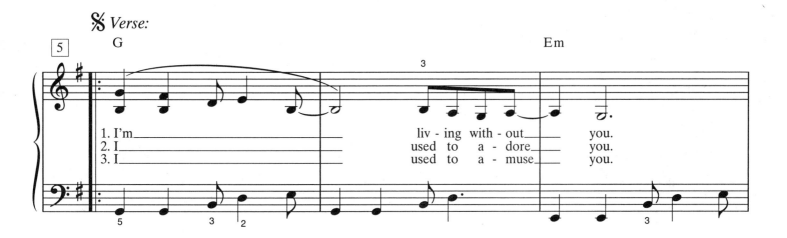

Special - 5 - 1

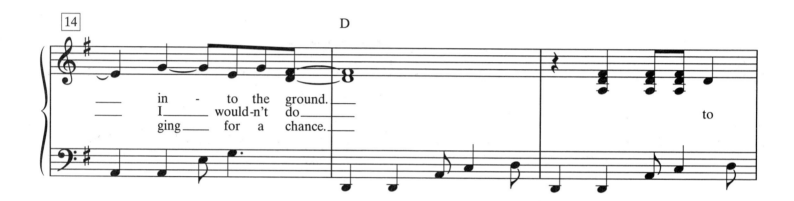

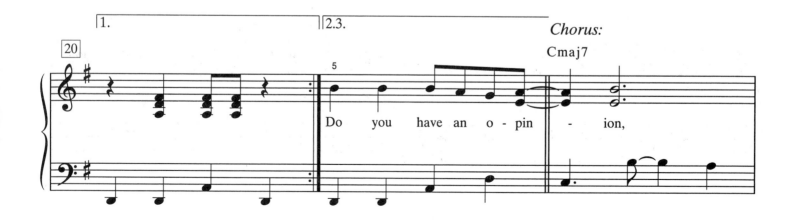

a mind of your own?

I thought you were spe -

cial.

I thought you should know.

To Coda ⊕

But I've run out of pa - tience.

I could-n't care less.

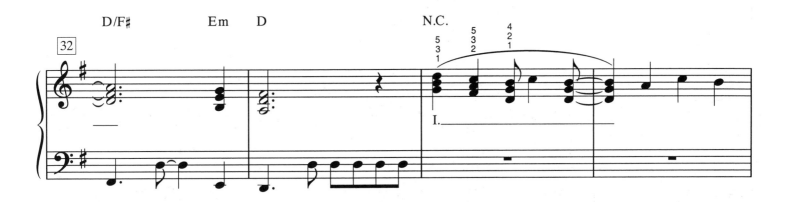

I.

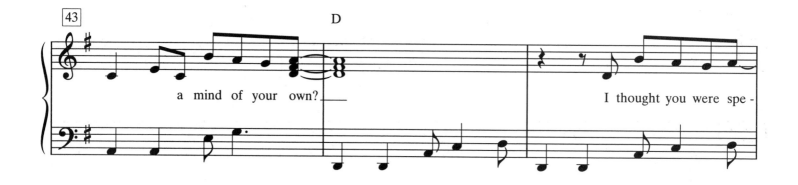

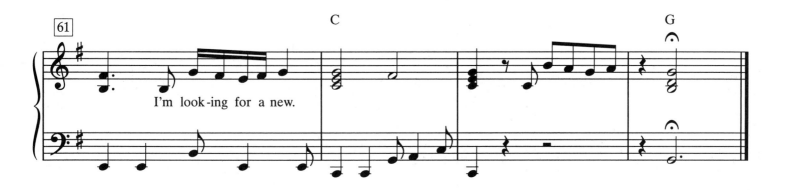

STAY THE SAME

Arranged by
JOHN BRIMHALL

Words and Music by
JOEY McINTYRE and
JOE CARRIER

Slowly ♩ = 72
Chorus:

Don't you ev - er wish you were some - one else.___ You were meant to be___ the

way you are, ex - act - ly. Don't you ev - er say___ you don't like the way you are. When you

learn to love your-self,___ you're bet - ter off by far. And I hope you'll al-ways stay the___

Stay the Same - 3 - 1

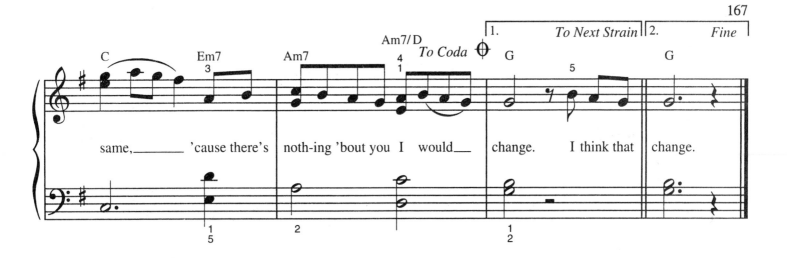

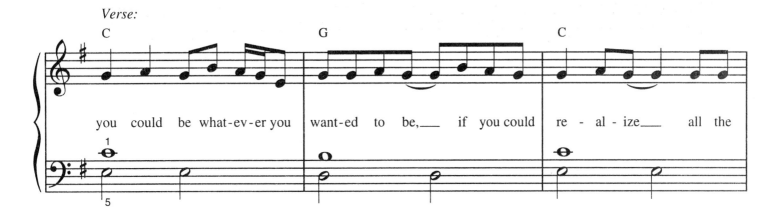

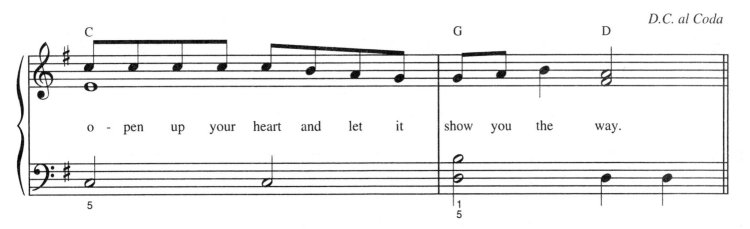

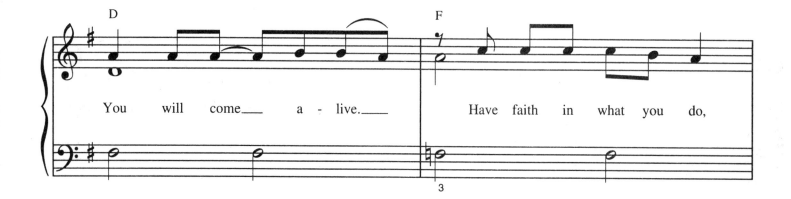

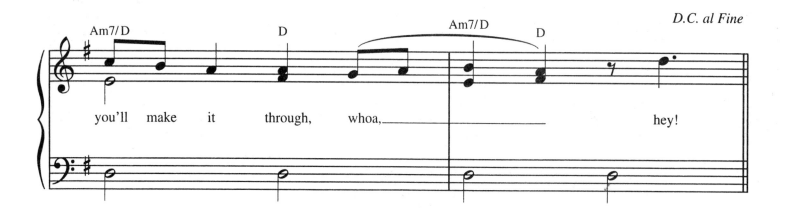

UNINVITED

Words and Music by
ALANIS MORISSETTE
Arranged by DAN COATES

Uninvited - 3 - 1

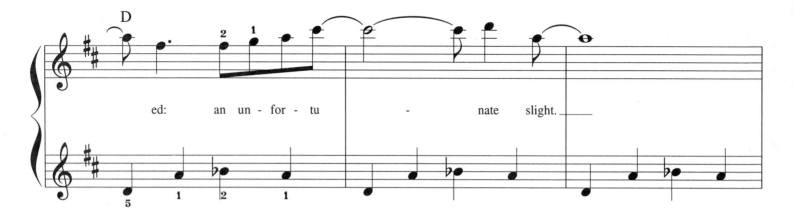

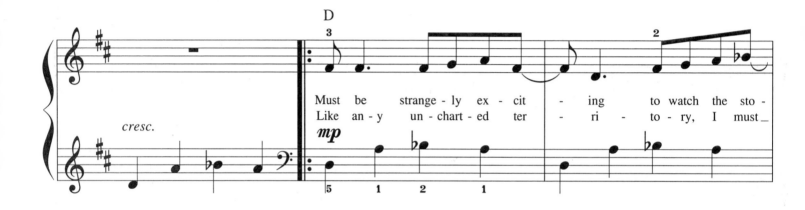

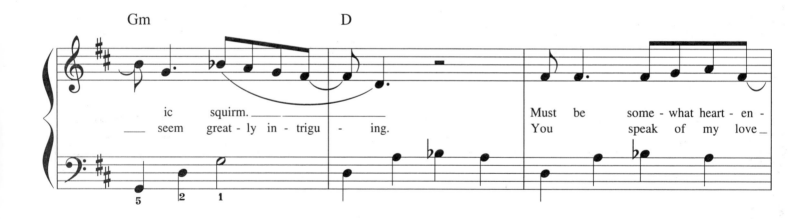

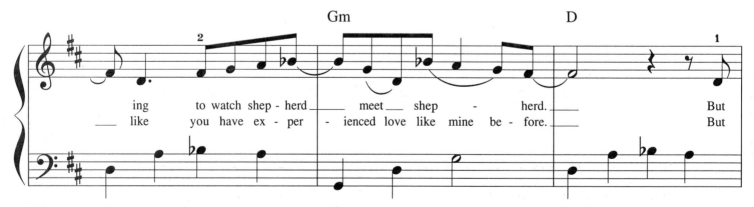

you,   you're not al - lowed; ___ you're un - in - vit - ed: an un - for - tu
this   is not al - lowed; ___ you're un - in - vit - ed: an un - for - tu

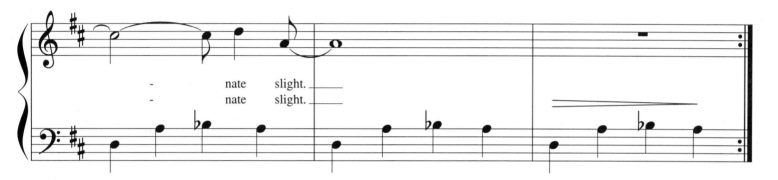

- nate   slight. ___
- nate   slight. ___

I   don't think you un - wor - thy;   I   need a mo -

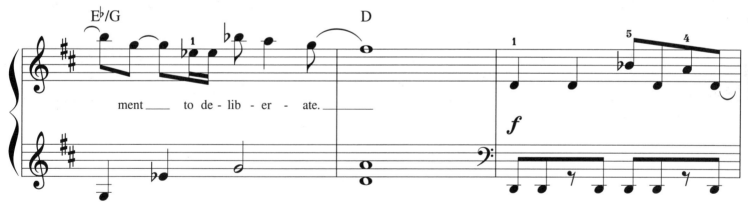

ment ___ to de - lib - er - ate. ___

STRONG ENOUGH

Words and Music by
MARK TAYLOR and
PAUL BARRY

Moderate dance beat (♩ = 132)

Verse 1:

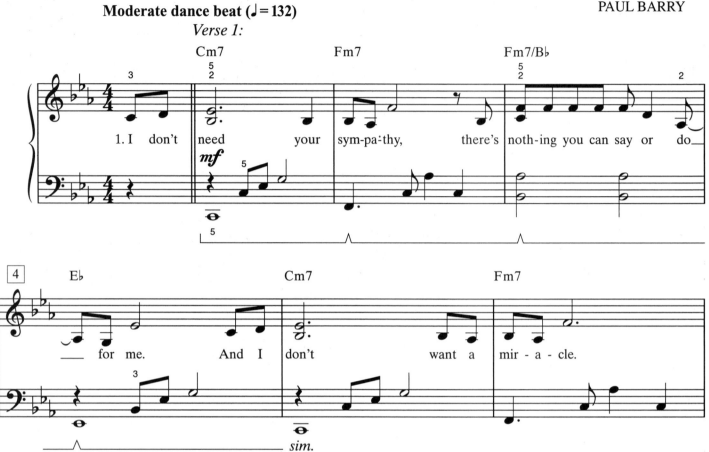

1. I don't need your sym-pa-thy, there's noth-ing you can say or do

for me. And I don't want a mir - a - cle.

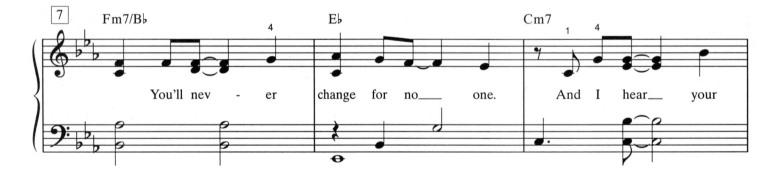

You'll nev - er change for no___ one. And I hear___ your

rea - sons why.___ Where did___ you sleep last night?___ And was___ she

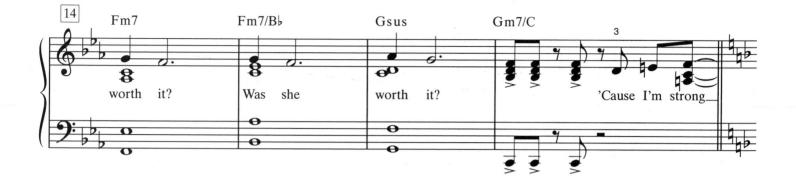

Chorus:

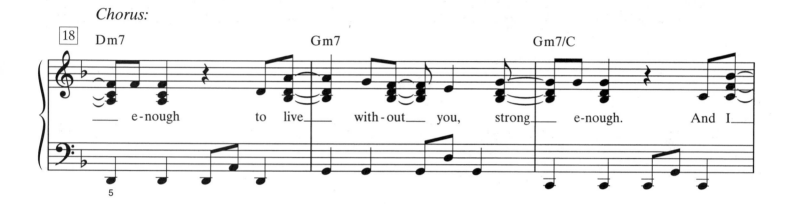

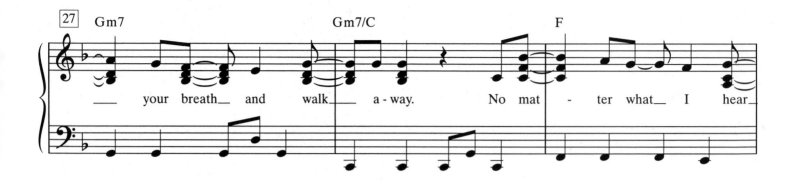

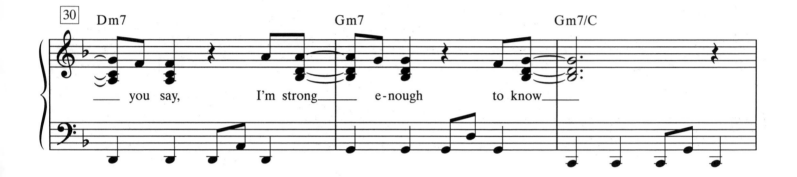

Verse 2:

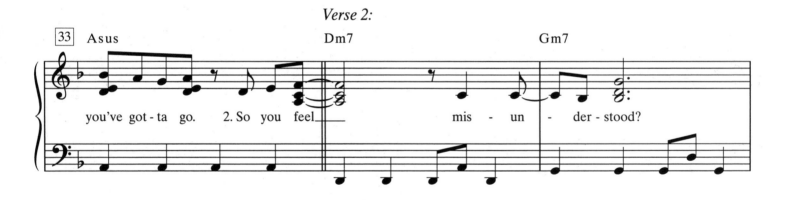

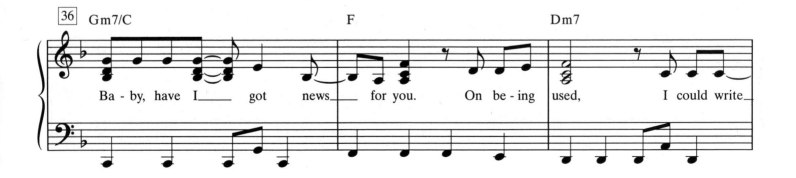

the book.

But you don't wan-na hear a-bout it.

'Cause I've been los - ing sleep, and you've been go -

in' cheap. And she ain't worth half of me, it's true.

Now I'm tell-ing you. Come hell or

176

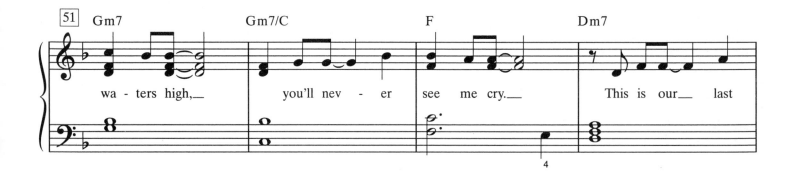

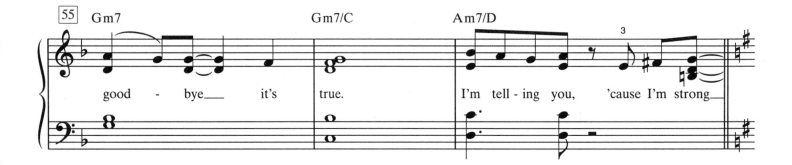

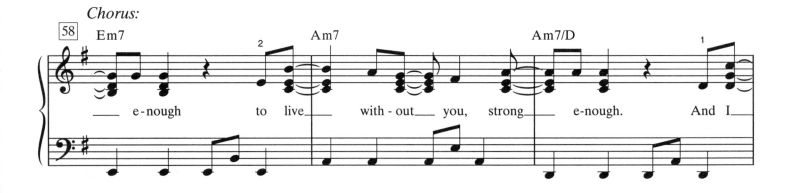

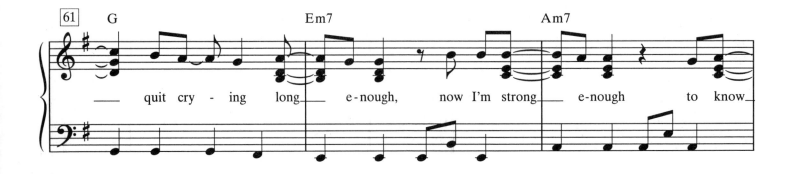

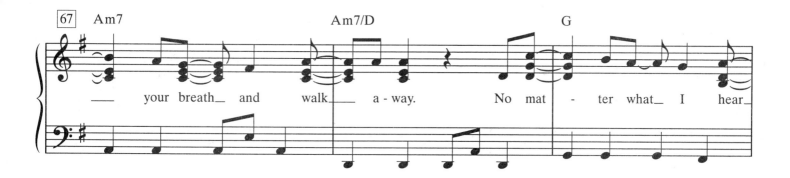

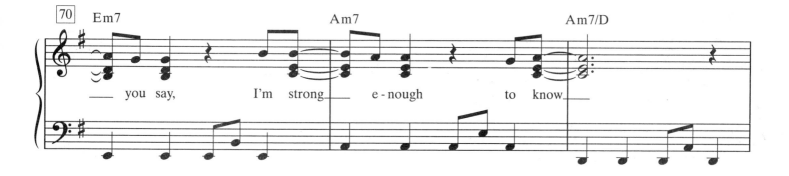

THANK U

Words by ALANIS MORISSETTE
Music by ALANIS MORISSETTE
and GLEN BALLARD

Moderately (♩ = 80)

※ Verse:

1. How 'bout get-ting off___ of these an - ti - bi - ot - ics.
2.3. *See additional lyrics*

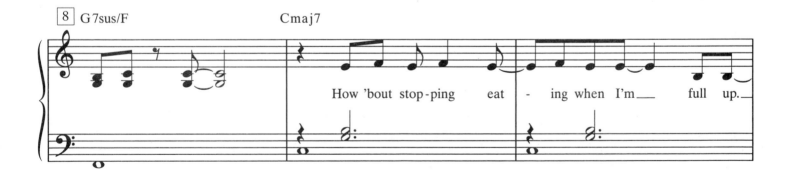

How 'bout stop-ping eat - ing when I'm___ full up.

Thank U - 4 - 1

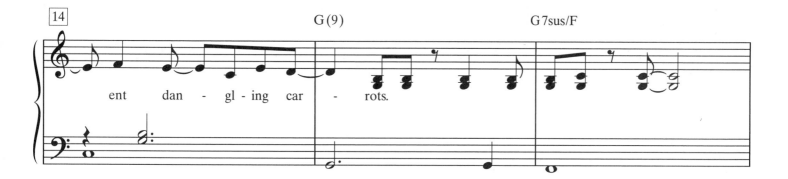

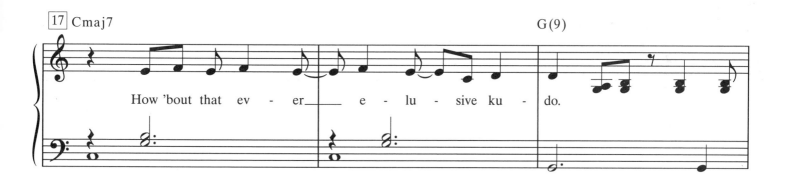

Chorus:

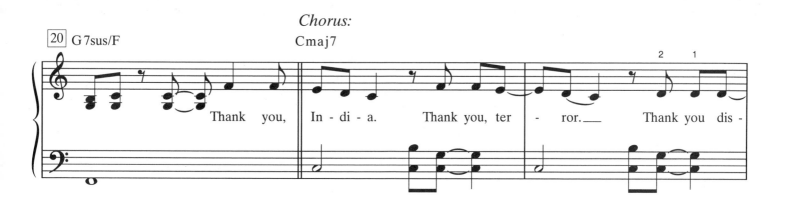

il - lu - sion - ment.___ Thank you, frail - ty. Thank you, con-

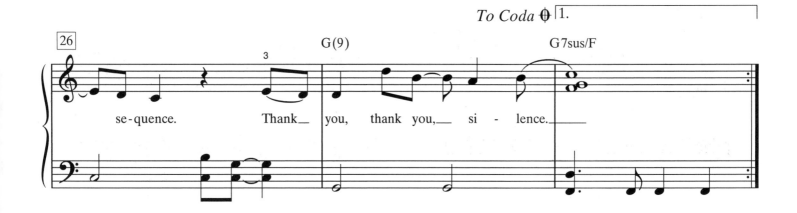

To Coda ⊕ 1.

se - quence. Thank___ you, thank you,___ si - lence.___

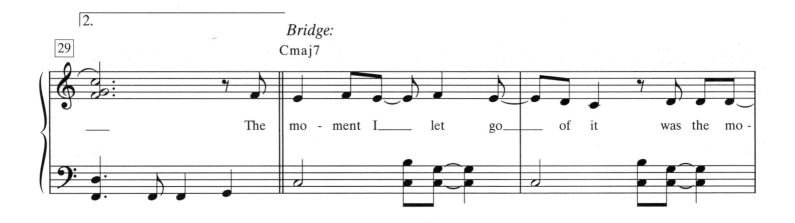

2.

Bridge:

___ The mo - ment I___ let go___ of it was the mo -

ment I got___ more than I could___ han - dle.___ The mo - ment___ I___ jumped off___

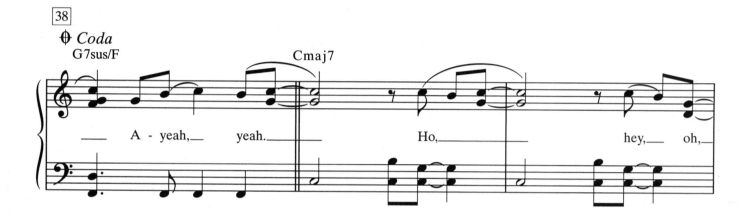

Verse 2:
How 'bout me not blaming you for everything.
How 'bout me enjoying the moment for once.
How 'bout how good it feels to finally forgive you.
How 'bout grieving it all one at a time.
(To Chorus:)

Verse 3:
How 'bout no longer being masochistic.
How 'bout remembering your divinity.
How 'bout unabashedly bawling your eyes out.
How 'bout not equating death with stopping.
(To Chorus:)

THAT DON'T IMPRESS ME MUCH

Arranged by
JOHN BRIMHALL

Words and Music by
SHANIA TWAIN and R.J. LANGE

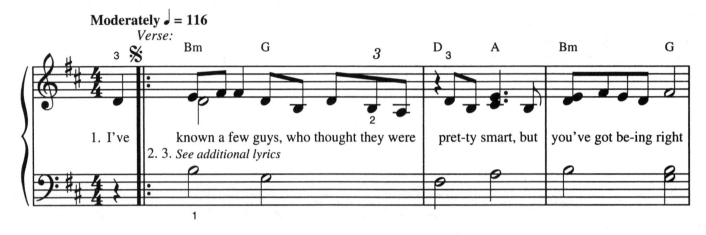

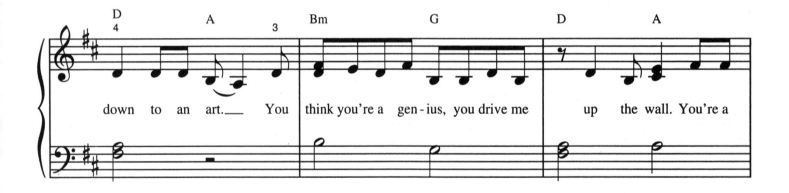

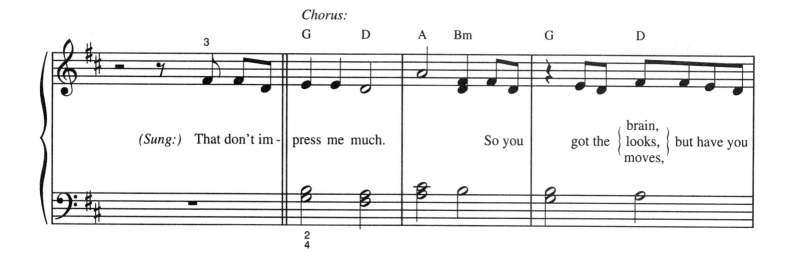

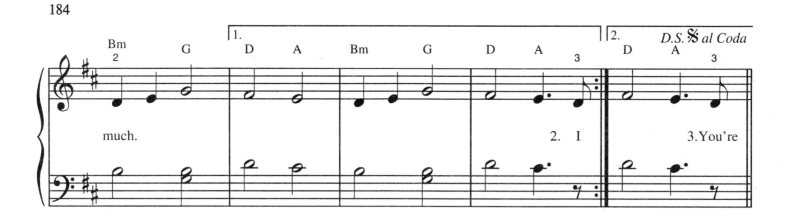

much.
2. I
3. You're

mid - dle of the night. That don't im - press me much.

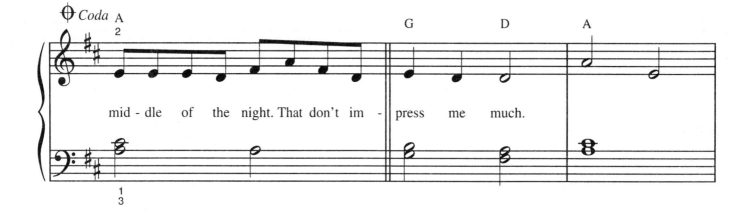

You think you're cool, but have you got the touch? Now, now don't get me wrong, yeah, I

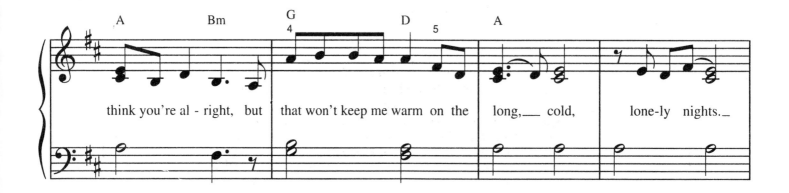

think you're al - right, but that won't keep me warm on the long,___ cold, lone - ly nights.___

That don't im - press____ me

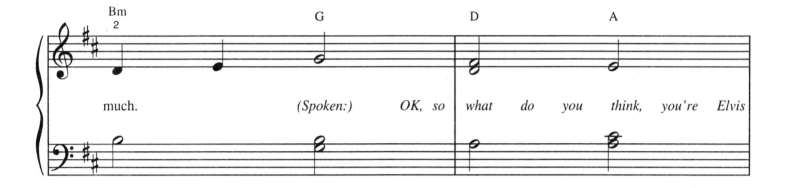

much. *(Spoken:)* OK, so *what do you think, you're Elvis*

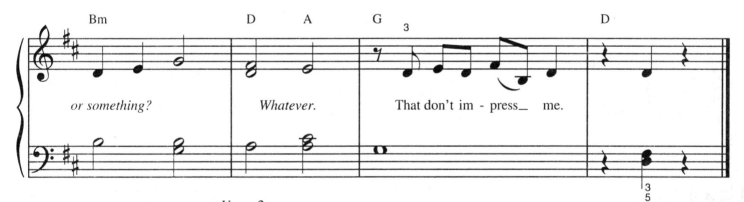

or something? *Whatever.* That don't im - press_ me.

Verse 2:
I never knew a guy who carried a mirror in his pocket
And a comb up his sleeve, just in case.
And all that extra-hold gel in your hair oughta lock it,
'Cause heaven forbid it should fall outta place.
Oh, oh, you think you're special.
Oh, oh, you think you're something else.
(Spoken:) OK, so you're Brad Pitt.
(To Chorus:)

Verse 3:
You're one of those guys who likes to shine his machine.
You make me take off my shoes before you let me get in.
I can't believe you kiss your car good-night.
Come on, baby, tell me, you must be jokin', right?
Oh, oh, you think you're special.
Oh, oh, you think you're something else.
(Spoken:) OK, so you've got a car.
(To Chorus:)

THAT'S THE WAY IT IS

Words and Music by
MAX MARTIN, KRISTIAN LUNDIN
and ANDREAS CARLSSON
Arranged by DAN COATES

Moderately slow, with a beat

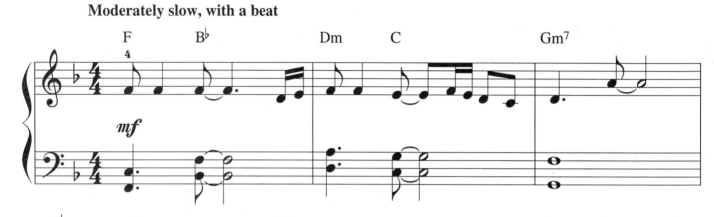

Verse:

That's the Way It Is - 4 - 1

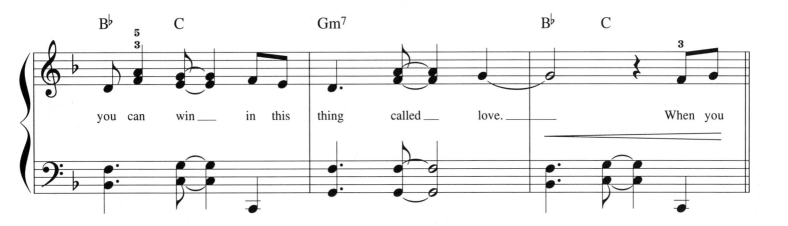

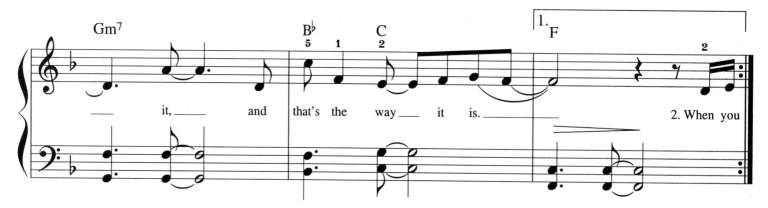

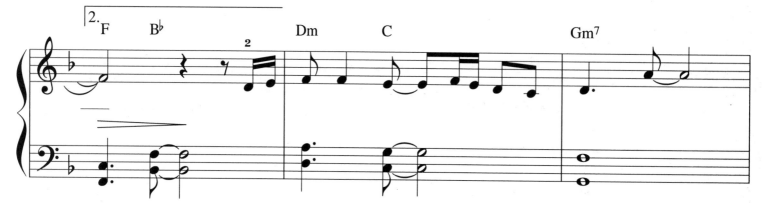

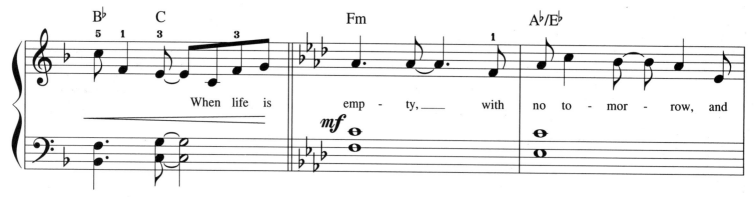

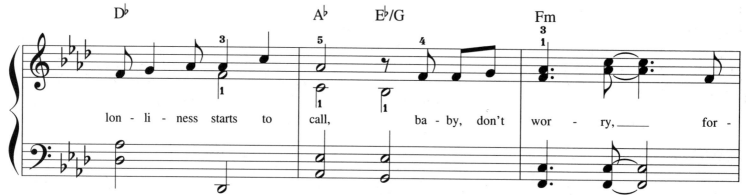

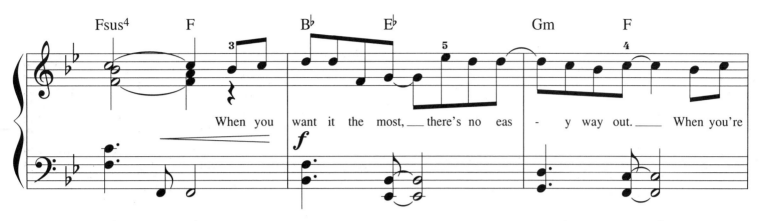

When you want it the most, ___ there's no eas - y way out. ___ When you're

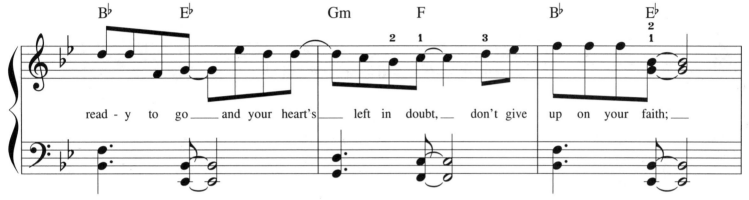

read - y to go ___ and your heart's ___ left in doubt, ___ don't give up on your faith; ___

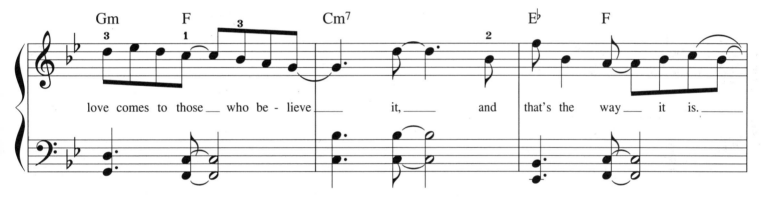

love comes to those ___ who be - lieve ___ it, ___ and that's the way ___ it is. ___

Don't give up on your faith; ___

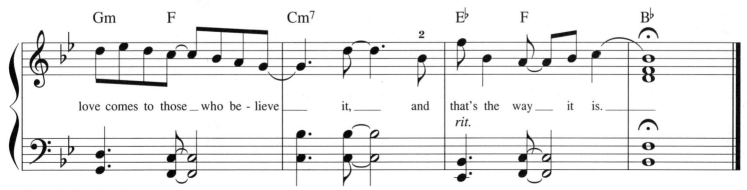

love comes to those ___ who be - lieve ___ it, ___ and that's the way ___ it is. ___

DAN COATES

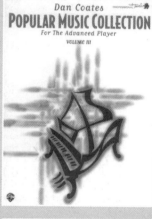
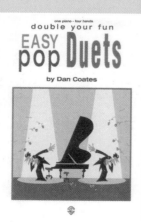
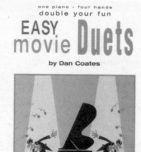

John Brimhall's
A DOZEN AND ONE
Series

This popular series from John Brimhall was designed to provide supplementary books to be used with any method book. Each book contains twelve easy piano arrangements, plus one bonus song. A fabulous addition to any pianist's library!

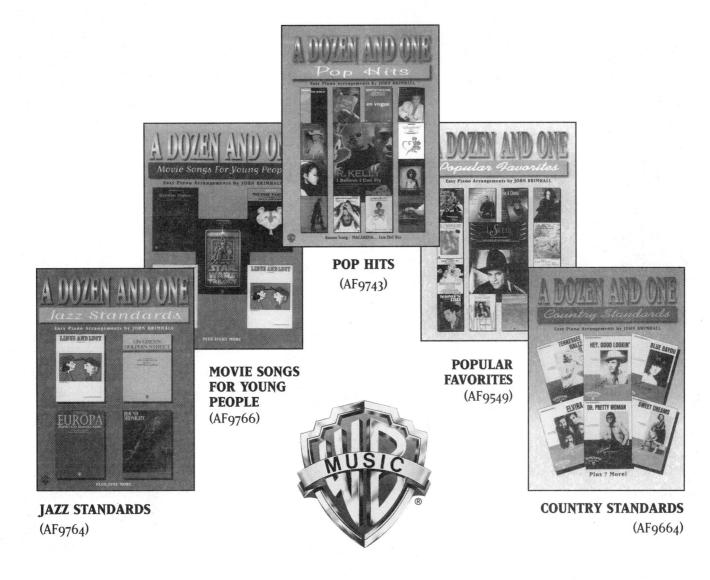

POP HITS
(AF9743)

MOVIE SONGS FOR YOUNG PEOPLE
(AF9766)

POPULAR FAVORITES
(AF9549)

JAZZ STANDARDS
(AF9764)

COUNTRY STANDARDS
(AF9664)

ALSO AVAILABLE

Academy Award Winning Songs
(AF9687)

Christmas Pops
(AF9830)

Old Time Rock and Roll Hits
(AF9816)

Popular Love Songs
(AF9834)

Soft Rock Hits
(AF9807)

Songs from Award Winning Broadway Shows
(AF9727)

AD0140

Intermediate/Advanced Piano Music
from
Dan Coates

Best in Standards (Revised), Book 2
(PF0542)
All the Way • Lullaby of Birdland • Secret Love • Sweet Georgia Brown • Three Coins in the Fountain • As Time Goes By • Misty • What's New? • Night and Day • That's All.

The Best of Broadway
(PF0871)
Creative arrangements of Broadway's very best from *Barnum, The Pajama Game, The Will Rogers Follies, City of Angels* and more. Titles include: The Colors of My Life • Corner of the Sky • Favorite Son • If My Friends Could See Me Now • My Unknown Someone • Send in the Clowns • She Loves Me.

Best of the '70s & '80s
(PF0768)
Arthur's Theme (Best That You Can Do) • Brian's Song • Come in from the Rain • How Do You Keep the Music Playing? • Hymne • If • I'll Still Be Loving You • One Moment in Time • The Rose • Saving All My Love for You and more.

The Best in Christmas Music Complete
(PF0735A)
Includes: Christmas Auld Lang Syne • The Christmas Waltz • God Rest Ye Merry Gentlemen • (There's No Place Like) Home for the Holidays • I Heard the Bells on Christmas Day • It Came Upon the Midnight Clear • Let It Snow! Let It Snow! Let It Snow! • Rockin' Around the Christmas Tree • Rudolph the Red-Nosed Reindeer and more.

The Best in Pops, Book 1
(PF0187)
Thirteen top hits including: Up Where We Belong • As Time Goes By • We've Got Tonight • How Do You Keep the Music Playing? • Chariots of Fire and many more.

The Best in Pops, Book 4
(PF0608)
Includes: Anne's Theme • Friends & Lovers (Both to Each Other) • Hymne • I'll Still Be Loving You • Kei's Song • Till I Loved You (Love Theme from *Goya*).

The Best in Pops, Book 5
(PF0756)
Alone in the World • Ashokan Farewell • The Colors of My Life • Get Here • The Gift of Love • (Everything I Do) I Do It for You • I Love to See You Smile • On My Way to You • Summer Me, Winter Me • When You Tell Me That You Love Me.

The Best in Popular Sheet Music
(AF9736)
Contains: Angel Eyes • Because You Loved Me • Desperado • From a Distance • The Greatest Love of All • (Everything I Do) I Do It for You • I Can Love You Like That • I Swear • If You Believe • Stairway to Heaven • Un-Break My Heart • Valentine and 10 more.

Dan Coates Popular Music Collection for the Advanced Player
(AF9555)
An advanced-level book that contains a dozen sophisticated arrangements, including: Angel Eyes • For Love Alone • The Greatest Love of All • I Can Love You Like That • I Swear • New York, New York • Over the Rainbow • The Rose • Tears in Heaven • Theme from *Love Affair* and more.

Dan Coates Popular Music Collection for the Advanced Player, Volume II
(AF9754)
A dozen challenging settings which will provide hours of pleasure for pianists at the advanced level. Includes: Because You Loved Me • Beauty and the Beast • Canon in D • Desperado • Hey, There • If You Believe • Send in the Clowns • Un-Break My Heart • Valentine.

Fantastic TV & Movie Songs (Revised Edition)
(PF0925)
Great television and movie music including: Anywhere the Heart Goes (Meggie's Theme) (from "The Thorn Birds") • Arthur's Theme (Best That You Can Do) (from *Arthur*) • Can You Read My Mind? (Love Theme from *Superman*) • Friends & Lovers (Both to Each Other) (from "Days of Our Lives") • The Rose (from *The Rose*) • Up Where We Belong (from *An Officer and a Gentleman*).

Great Piano Christmas Hits
(AF9681)
An advanced-level book that contains 20 sophisticated Dan Coates arrangements, including: Away in a Manger • Deck the Halls • God Rest Ye Merry Gentlemen • Hark! The Herald Angels Sing • It Came Upon the Midnight Clear • Merry Christmas Darling • Rockin' Around the Christmas Tree • Silent Night • Sleigh Ride.

Great Popular Music of the '80s
(PF0621)
Contains: Always on My Mind • Can't Fight This Feeling • Hymne • I'll Still Be Loving You • Nothing's Gonna Change My Love for You • Once Before I Go • The Search Is Over • We Are the World • The Wind Beneath My Wings and more.

Great Popular Piano Hits, Volume 2
(F3050P9X)
Eight beautiful intermediate piano arrangements of some of our most popular titles like: Corner of the Sky • Didn't We • The Entertainer • The Greatest Love of All • Three Times a Lady • You Light Up My Life.

I Just Can't Stop Loving You & 16 Romantic Ballads
(PF0940)
The ever-popular Dan Coates provides the intermediate to advanced player with creative melodic arrangements of some of today's most enduring love songs. Selections include: As Time Goes By • The Homecoming • Misty • That's What Friends Are For • Up Where We Belong • We've Got Tonight and many more.

My All-Time Favorite Melodies
(PF0824)
All the Way • Alone in the World • Ashokan Farewell • Brian's Song • Color the Children • The Homecoming • How Do You Keep the Music Playing? • If • In Finding You, I Found Love • Misty • Theme from *Nicholas and Alexandra* • The Rose • Time in a Bottle • We've Got Tonight • The Wind Beneath My Wings and more.

The New Dan Coates Professional Touch Encyclopedia (Revised)
(PF0562B)
Includes: Saving All My Love for You • Separate Lives (Love Theme from *White Nights*) • That's What Friends Are For • Send in the Clowns • Open Arms • (Everything I Do) I Do It for You • Up Where We Belong • The Wind Beneath My Wings • Eye of the Tiger • I Swear • The Rose • Stairway to Heaven and much more.

The Rose & 49 Top Professional Touch Hits
(PF0826A)
Anne's Theme • As Time Goes By • Can You Read My Mind? • Evergreen • From a Distance • I Just Can't Stop Loving You • Nothing's Gonna Change My Love for You • One Moment in Time • Send in the Clowns • We Are the World • What's New? and more.

The Wind Beneath My Wings and 9 Piano Solos
(PF0698)
Includes: Can You Read My Mind? (Love Theme from *Superman*) • How Do You Keep the Music Playing? • Hymne • Kei's Song • Miss Celie's Blues (Sister) • Missing (Theme from *Missing*) • Noelle's Theme (The Other Side of Midnight) • Once Before I Go • One Moment in Time and title song.